STUDIES IN ROMANCE LANGUAGES: 20

THE TRAGIC MYTH

Lorca and *Cante Jondo*

Edward F. Stanton

THE UNIVERSITY PRESS OF KENTUCKY

Some of the material in this book has been treated previously in *Hispania,
Romanische Forschungen,* and *South Atlantic Bulletin.*

Stanton, Edward F   1942-
   The tragic myth.

   (Studies in Romance languages; 20)
   Bibliography: p.
   Includes index.
   1. García Lorca, Federico, 1898-1936—Knowledge—Music.
2. Flamenco. I. Title. II. Series.
PQ6613.A763Z8857   861'.6'2   77-84067
ISBN 0-8131-1378-4

Scholarly publisher for the Commonwealth
serving Berea College, Centre College of Kentucky,
Eastern Kentucky University, The Filson Club,
Georgetown College, Kentucky Historical Society,
Kentucky State University, Morehead State University,
Murray State University, Northern Kentucky University,
Transylvania University, University of Kentucky,
University of Louisville, and Western Kentucky University.

Editorial and Sales Offices: Lexington, Kentucky 40506

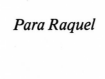

Para Raquel

Contents

Prologue

It is surprising that nobody has treated in depth the subject of Federico García Lorca and *cante jondo*, or flamenco, the traditional music of his native Andalusia. With literature, music constituted the most important activity of his life. The two arts were closely related to each other throughout his career. As a child, Lorca imbibed traditional Andalusian songs from the lips of the family maids, whom he would remember with affection years later. At a very early age he began to study piano, and during his adolescence, music and poetry competed for primacy among his interests. His first book was dedicated to his music teacher, who instilled in him a love for the world of art and creation.

At first Lorca's interests followed the path of classical music. But as he gradually drew away from a serious study of the piano and devoted himself to literature, he returned to the world of traditional music he had known as a child on the Granadine *vega*. At the same time, he left the effusions of his youthful verse behind and turned toward a more popular inspiration. These were the years in which composers of classical music— Falla, Bartók, Stravinsky—were beginning to experiment with folk rhythms, melodies, and harmonies in their larger compositions. In 1922, Lorca, Falla and others organized the famous "Concurso del Cante Jondo" in Granada, the most important event in the modern history of this music. To foment interest in the competition, the poet gave an inspired lecture. During this same period he wrote his *Poema del cante jondo,* though it was not published until several years later.

From this point on, all of Lorca's musical activity was devoted to Spanish folk songs. Never a mere regionalist, he studied anthologies compiled in all parts of the Peninsula and collected ballads from regions other than Andalusia. He incorporated pieces from the medieval and Renaissance *Cancioneros* into the classic Spanish plays he directed as head of an itinerant, nonprofessional theater group, "La Barraca." He also harmonized a dozen or so folk songs which are popular to this day. They come from various parts of Spain, but the most characteristic are probably those he heard as a child in the Granadine countryside. In addition, Lorca composed original pieces for his own plays. His drama could be seen as a modern continuation of Spain's Golden Age theater, with its popular inspiration and fusion of plastic, musical, and dramatic elements. He also liked the *zarzuela* or Spanish light opera when performed in good taste; it too descends from the classical drama. Just as he was attracted to Golden Age theater and the opera, Lorca was inevitably drawn to *cante jondo*. The joining of singer, dancer, musician, and public approached the ideal of a composite art form for which he sought expression all his life.

In the mythic dimension of *cante jondo* and Lorca's poetry, I have found the central parallel between these two manifestations of Andalusian art—one ancient and traditional, the other personal and modern. As we shall see, the origins of *cante jondo* are lost in a mist of legend. This music did not appear in written history until the eighteenth century, but its roots reach back to ancient times. The *saeta* or Passion song, for example, seems to represent a modern survival of pre-Christian seasonal rites. The incantatory power of flamenco music, its association with a ritual of dance, and the Dionysian nature of its inspiration have suggested mythic origins to several observers. In his lectures and poetry based on *cante jondo*, Lorca showed himself to be fully aware of these origins. Gustavo Correa, Juan López-Morillas, and other critics have discussed the mythic elements in his work; here I am concerned only with those elements that can be clarified by a comparison with *cante jondo*.

In general, we could say that Lorca's poetry carries us back to a mythic universe. The word myth appears in Aristotle's *Poetics* in reference to plot, action, or fable. The "plot" of Lorca's verse, like that of *cante jondo*, is essentially tragic. It unfolds under the auspices of *duende*—demon, muse, or inspiration—which reveals itself in the expression of death and suffering. In both Lorca and flamenco, the scenery of this tragic fable is Andalusia. Not the concrete area of southern Spain, but a poetic region of the mind. As in ancient myth, this realm is characterized by a constant interaction between man and nature, man and the cosmos. Here we recognize what Cassirer called the "consanguinity of all forms of life," Lévy-Brühl's "participation."

The characteristic inhabitants of Lorca's Andalusia are the gypsies; they have always been the best interpreters of *cante jondo*. In the magic of word and rhythm, through the use of archetypal images, through metaphor and symbol, the poet evokes the primitive imagination of this wandering people. The gypsies probably possess a system of beliefs that attempts to explain the phenomena of nature and life—a kind of racial mythology. With a few exceptions, Lorca did not explore these concrete stories and legends. In the true mythical imagination, there is implied an act of belief—whether in the ancient Greeks or the primitive peoples of today. This is what distinguishes myth in the gypsies and Aeschylus, for example, from its use by modern authors. Poetry is not exactly synonymous with myth, though both derive from the same human needs, represent a similar kind of symbolic formulation, and invest experience with the same sense of awe and wonder. At its best, Lorca's art carries us back to a primal world where intuition prevails over reason, and where the whole range of verbal and musical expression—religion, myth, poetry—arises from a common impulse.

In part I of this study, I have examined Lorca's theoretical and practical approach to *cante jondo*, as seen in his lectures on the subject and in the 1922 concurso. In part II, I have searched for direct and—far more important—indirect echoes of this music in his work. Certain basic motifs and themes are common to both Lorca's poetry and the world of flamenco: *pena negra,* the Andalusian sense of pain and suffering; the guitar; the bull and bullfighting. In part III, I have explored the mythic quality of the poet's art in relation to *cante jondo*. I have found the central parallel between the poet's work and *cante jondo* in what could be called the tragic myth. Andalusia, the gypsy, and the *saeta* reveal the mythic roots of this music as interpreted by Lorca.

A word on the title: I have followed Lorca's own usage in employing the denomination *cante jondo* rather than flamenco, which is much more current outside of Spain. When Lorca was alive, the traditional music of Andalusia was in critical danger of corruption and extinction. It became imperative to make a clear differentiation between the authentic, ancient song, *cante jondo*, and its impure modern progeny, flamenco. Thanks to the zeal of Lorca, his friend Manuel de Falla, and others like them, the battle against extinction has been won. It is no longer necessary to use the select vocabulary of an elite. Because the term *cante jondo* has the advantage of being specific in referring to the more serious, "deep" genres of this music—the only ones that mattered to Lorca—and out of respect for the poet's own preference, I have employed it in the title and predominantly in the text. I have also used the denomination flamenco occasionally; it is more generic and sanctioned by general usage. Terms like *cante jondo, cante grande,* and *cante chico* imply a value judgment and are somewhat subjective. Moreover, the important thing here is not the song itself, but the singer who interprets it. A light song performed by a great *cantaor* is more moving than a serious song performed by a poor singer.

Though they have much in common, we should not make the mistake of identifying Lorca's poetry with *cante jondo.* Both are supreme expressions of Spanish and Andalusian culture, but they remain substantially different. One is highly refined and individual, the other traditional and collective. At the center of a great artist's creation we see an enormous number of converging possibilities for analysis. My approach has been confined to one of these possibilities in Lorca's work: *cante jondo.* Choosing only one, we proclaim the richness of art and the limits of our method.

I. Theory and Practice

Chapter One

Theory: The Lectures

Perhaps the best way to enter the world of García Lorca and *cante jondo* would be to look at the poet's lectures on the subject. They will serve as an introduction to the traditional music of Andalusia, at the same time revealing Lorca's attitude towards it. This is an indispensable preliminary to a reading of his poetry from the point of view of *cante jondo*.

THE PRIMITIVE ANDALUSIAN SONG

In early 1922, Lorca wrote and delivered a major lecture in preparation for the "Concurso del Cante Jondo" in June of that year.[1] Its purpose was to create interest in the approaching competition and to reveal the prevailing decadence of *cante jondo*. For nearly half a century, the traditional music of southern Spain had suffered from the plague of commercialization. The music had emigrated to the theater and *café chantant* of the cities from its breeding grounds in the country and small towns. In the popular mind it began to be associated with a world of vice and braggadocio. Every day that passed, warned Lorca, a leaf was falling from the noble tree of Andalusian lyricism. The time had come for poets, musicians, and artists to join forces and save this musical treasure.

Openly recognizing his debt to the theories of Manuel de Falla in this lecture, Lorca makes the distinction between *cante jondo* and flamenco. They are basically different in antiquity, structure, and spirit. Falla considered *cante jondo* to be an example of primitive music, the oldest in Europe; its roots probably go back to the ancient songs of India. The melodies progress by undulations of semitones, nearly impossible to represent on the rigid staff of our diatonic scale. As an expression of primitive music, it approaches the singing of birds and the "natural sounds of water and the forest."[2] Flamenco, on the other hand, is a modern development or corruption of *cante jondo*; it did not acquire a definite form until the eighteenth century. Its melodies move by leaps and follow the steps of the Western scale within the framework of a fixed rhythm.

The *siguiriya gitana* is taken by Lorca to be the most direct descendant of primitive Andalusian music, and its ideal model.[3] He cites Falla's affirmation that it is the only song in Europe which has preserved the essences of ancient Oriental music. No other regional song can be compared to it in poetic quality, and "rarely, very rarely, does the human spirit achieve works of such a nature" (I: 976). It should not be considered a mere transplant of Oriental music in Spain, since it has an unmistakable individuality of its own. At the most, it may have developed from the grafting of Eastern influences onto the stem of Iberian tradition. According to Falla and Lorca, three major historical factors have contributed to the growth of the *siguiriya* and its related forms: the Byzantine liturgy used by the Spanish Church until the adoption of the Roman rite in the eleventh century; the Arab presence in the Peninsula from 714 to 1492; and the arrival of the gypsies in Spain toward the middle of the fifteenth century. The reaction of these forces on the native music of Andalusia—which is largely unknown—created what we now know as *cante jondo*.

The most striking similarities between the *siguiriya* and Byzantine chant, Lorca continues, are the use of primitive tonal modes and the absence of a definite rhythmic pattern. He skims over the idea of Arabic influence, merely pointing out that many folk songs of Morocco, Algeria, and Tunisia are still known in those countries as "music of the Moors from Granada." But he is much more specific in his treatment of the gypsy element in the *siguiriya gitana*. The very name of the song and the Romany words in its verses are a testimony to the influence of this nomadic people. But the gypsies did not invent *cante jondo*, and it is not performed in the other countries inhabited by them. They probably found many qualities in native Andalusian music that were compatible with their own artistic sensibility, and thus became its best interpreters. In the process, they must have contributed something to the songs.

Still following Falla, Lorca accepts the idea of the gypsies' Indian origin. About 1400 they probably left India in flight from Mongol invaders. Twenty years later they had reached Europe, Lorca says, and could have entered Spain aboard the Saracen ships that plied along the Mediterranean coasts.[4] The gypsies bore a millennial artistic tradition and through it *cante jondo* absorbed some of the elements of Hindu chant: modulation by semitones; a reduced melodic range; and the almost obsessive repetition of a single note—a technique common to certain forms of incantation. Thus the *siguiriya* often gives the impression of a musical prose with no fixed rhythm, even though its verses consist of assonant tercets and quatrains. At certain places determined by the sense of the text, the singer employs elaborate vocal inflections which seem to be ornaments but are actually an integral part of the melody. According to Lorca, it is to the gypsies that we owe these complex and emotive songs: the "soul of our soul. . . . lyrical channels through which escape all the suffering and ritual gestures of our race" (I: 979).

When he discusses *cante jondo* as poetry, Lorca is on much surer ground. Sometimes these verses achieve a remarkable suggestiveness with the most economical of means. As in all great poetry, the basic themes are pain, suffering, love, and death:

> Cerco tiene la luna
> mi amor ha muerto.

There is no middle road; this is a poetry of extremes. The refined, civilized emotions of nostalgia, ennui, and love of nature find no place here. "The Andalusian either cries to the stars or kisses the reddish dust of his roads" (I: 984). The emotion is so overwhelming that it leaves no room for the description of nature. In fact the poetry of *cante jondo* could be called nocturnal; like a nightingale, it sings blindly in the dark. It contains no morning or afternoon, no mountains or plains. This concentration and absence of description gives it intensity and depth. Anything beyond the bare and simple emotion would be superfluous. Yet we should not assume that nature is totally absent from these verses. It never appears for its own sake, but may be portrayed in relation to the poet's feelings. Lorca refers to the pantheism of this poetry. The air, sea, earth, and moon may be consulted for their divinatory powers:

> En mitá der "má"
> había una piedra
> y se sentaba mi compañerita
> a contarle sus penas.

The materialization of the wind is a recurrent motif; the element may console a desperate lover:

> Subí a la muralla;
> me respondió el viento:

¿para qué tantos suspiritos
si ya no hay remedio?

Pain or suffering take on a personality and are incarnated in the form of a dark and tragic woman. Crying and tears represent another example of this tendency for emotions to become embodied in a concrete form. Lorca points out that the poetry of *cante jondo* is predominantly anonymous. When learned poets—Salvador Rueda and Manuel Machado—have turned their hands to it, the results have nearly always been fatal. The heavy accent of the "man who knows grammar" is evident from the first. One should not try to take more than the ultimate essences from the people, and perhaps a few characteristic brushstrokes, Lorca says. We should never attempt to imitate their creations, because all we do is muddle them (I: 986).

Just as the *siguiriya* shows some characteristics of Eastern music, the poetry of *cante jondo* has an affinity with certain Eastern—especially Arabic—verse. Lorca confines himself to a rather general comparison here. The praise of wine, the obsession with women's hair, and crying are a few of the common themes. In both *cante jondo* and Arabic poetry, the only defense against the ravages of time is love. Though it always brings suffering in its wake, love is stronger than death.

Lorca concludes his lecture with a salute to the *cantaor* or singer. His art is a solemn rite, to be approached with profound religious respect. More than a performer, the *cantaor* becomes a kind of medium through which the history and suffering of the race are expressed. The singers of the deepest genres have usually been men, since they alone can bear the immense emotional thrust required in performance. "The *siguiriya* is like a hot iron that burns the heart, throat and lips of those who pronounce it" (I: 993).

In 1932 Lorca gave his only other lecture on the exclusive theme of Andalusian music.[5] It adds very little to the first, from which it lifts whole passages verbatim. But the poet did make two important additions. Whereas he had been silent about a possible Jewish influence before, he now suggests that certain Sephardic rhythms may have been assimilated in *cante jondo*.[6] He also discusses the role of the guitar in accompanying the singer. According to Lorca, the instrument's proper function is to give the song a rhythmic and harmonic background; the player should follow the singer and not attempt to display his own virtuosity. In contrast to the closed and circular melodic structure of Western music, the *siguiriya* is open and linear, potentially endless, like an arabesque. But when the guitar began to be used in conjunction with the voice in flamenco music, this loose melodic structure had to mold itself to the tonal patterns of the instrument. A proof of this theory is that the genres without accompaniment, such as *martinetes* and *saetas*, have a different melodic framework—freer but less logical. Lorca says that the guitar has ordered and enriched the dark and inarticulate muse of ancient Eastern music.

It would be an error to consider the poet's lectures as scholarly works. They are above all impassioned, lyrical outcries against the perils in which *cante jondo* found itself at the time. The theoretical content of these lectures was frankly based on a work by Manuel de Falla.[7] Lorca reelaborated the maestro's concepts for the benefit of a general audience. The technical strengths and weaknesses of his lectures are therefore those of the composer.

Falla's work may still be the best treatment of the theoretical origins of *cante jondo*,[8] but precisely because these origins are so ancient and obscure, his hypotheses are perforce vague and general. Falla's notion of Byzantine influence, for example, has never been clarified. Nearly everyone accepts the possibility of Jewish and Arabic influences, yet nobody has gone very far to elucidate them. The apparent similarities between *cante jondo* and the religious chant of the Middle East strike our ears at once, yet this initial impression cannot be verified with facts. The modern consensus seems to be that a flamenco substrate, composed of native Andalusian, Arabic, and Hebrew elements, already existed in southern Spain when the gypsies arrived there.[9] This substrate would correspond to the current of popular Andalusian poetry postulated years ago by Julián Ribera, and confirmed by later research.[10]

We should bear in mind that medieval poetry was created to be sung, music and verse forming integral components of the same art. Perhaps the Mozarabic *jarchas* offer an example of this latent substrate. They are the refrains of Arabic and Hebrew poems written in Andalusia between the eleventh and fourteenth centuries, possibly earlier. Their texts are in Mozarabic, the archaic dialect spoken by Christians in Moorish Spain. Several qualities of these little poems seem to foreshadow *cante jondo*: a popular air; concentration and intensity; concrete, sensual imagery; a frequently nocturnal atmosphere; a dwelling on love and suffering; abundant use of diminutives. Yet there exists no demonstrable link between the *jarchas* and flamenco, which did not appear in history until several hundred years later. The general belief is that *cante jondo* came into being when the gypsies absorbed the Andalusian substrate of music and poetry, enriching it with their own artistic tradition. But we have no record of this hypothetical period of assimilation. It is only in the late eighteenth century, under Carlos III, when Spanish folklore began to be conscious of itself, that we can start to document the growth of this music. Falla and Lorca remain silent about this entire modern period, since for them it was synonymous with commercialization and decadence.

Leaving Falla's theories for the moment, let us look at the recorded history of *cante jondo*, which has been divided into four major phases. (1) From the era of Carlos III until the middle of the nineteenth century, traditional music flourished in southern Spain. During this period the *siguiriya* and other songs preferred by Falla and Lorca must have acquired more or less definitive forms. (2) It was only in the second half of the last century that this music left the intimacy of private celebrations to become part of the public domain. This is the era of the first real professional singers and of the *café chantant*, a small and dimly lit locale with tables placed around an elevated stage.[11] Here the performers became known to the public in what has been called the "golden age" of *cante jondo*. But side by side with the pure forms, circumstantial couplets were sung in a mock style; some interpreters added ornaments of an operatic virtuosity. After 1870, the term flamenco began to be applied to both the music and the dance.[12] (3) By the early part of our century, the *cante* had borrowed elements from the *zarzuela* as well as the opera, thus becoming part of a theatrical spectacle. This was the phase of development known directly by Falla and the other Spanish writers who inveighed against it at one time or another: Baroja, Unamuno, and above all Eugenio Noel. (4) With the eventful Concurso del Cante Jondo of 1922, the revival of Andalusian music began, the last and present phase of its modern history.

Though Falla and Lorca were justified in despising the superficiality of much flamenco music in the nineteenth century, perhaps they failed to recognize the positive contributions of this period. Like prodigal sons, we may tend to disparage the century that has given us most of our institutions in their present form—the good and the bad together, often mingled and inseparable. The commercialization and professionalism of this music went hand in hand with its expansion and refinement; the epoch of the worst abuses was also that of the greatest achievements. Some of the singers most admired by Lorca made enormous fortunes with their voices:

Juan Breva, Silverio Franconetti, and Pastora Pavón, "Niña de los Peines." Professionalism was not necessarily synonymous with corruption.

A fundamental misconception may lie behind the composer's and the poet's prejudice against this period of growth and expansion. A basic premise of their theories is that *cante jondo* constitutes an expression of the people, a kind of musical folk art. This is not exactly correct. It differs from other traditional music in its technical complexity. The *cantaor* must undergo long and intense training to master his art, though the method is largely informal. His listeners deservedly regard him with a semireligious awe; the emotion he evokes in them occasionally resembles a mystic ecstasy.[13] The lyrical setting of the poetic texts is more urban than rural in contrast to the folk music of other countries and the rest of Spain. In the early 1800s several styles were still sung by the people in the Andalusian country and mountains—*temporeras, verdiales, serranas.* During the last hundred years, they have practically disappeared. *Cante jondo* is now without question a music of cities and towns; it belongs to a minority, not to the masses. It has probably always been "cryptic, occult, secret."[14] Nevertheless, it does possess some of the characteristics of traditional music: oral transmission, anonymous origin of music and verses, and largely illiterate performers who come from the fringes of society.

In spite of the theoretical misconceptions he inherited from Falla, Lorca's first lecture is probably the most evocative prose ever written about *cante jondo.* In all fairness to the composer, we should remember that he was more successful expressing the spirit of this music in his compositions than in prose. Perhaps Falla—in contrast to the poet—never had the openness and flexibility of character required to penetrate directly into the flamenco world.

In selecting the examples that illustrate his lecture, Lorca showed an infallible instinct for winnowing the best poetry from the abundant chaff. It must be admitted that many of the verses of *cante jondo* are mediocre or outright doggerel rendered tolerable by the incantatory power of the music. But the poetry can be superb, as in many of Lorca's examples.

The relation between the composition of this lecture and the *Poema del cante jondo* must have been close. Both were written around the time of the 1922 concurso, though the book was not published until 1931. Lorca used some similar imagery in lecture and verse. Indeed, it is partly as poetry that we should read his prose. Lorca confessed his lecture was poorly constructed. We have seen that it contains no original ideas, yet few writers have suggested the hidden essences of *cante jondo* as he does here. It is rightly called "deep" song, he tells us, because it is "deeper than all the wells and all the seas that surround the world, much deeper than the present heart that creàtes it and the voice that sings it, because it is almost infinite. It comes from distant races, crossing the cemetery of the years . . ." (I: 982). Beneath the verses a question throbs, he says, a terrible question without an answer. Life is seen through an impenetrable veil, as if through the eyes of an ancient sibyl or an Andalusian sphinx. Here we see the first glimmerings of an association between *cante jondo* and myth, which Lorca would develop in his next lecture and in his poetry.

THE THEORY OF *DUENDE*

Sometime after 1928, Lorca delivered a lecture that may contain his most inspired prose. "Teoría y juego del duende" (I: 1067-79) is essential for understanding his poetics and his attitude toward the music of his native region. This lecture does not deal exclusively with *cante jondo* as such, but is based on an idea from the world of flamenco: *duende*. The most common opinion is that this word derives from the Latin *domitus:* domestic or familiar spirit.[15] Its basic meaning is "inspiration" in the root sense, yet no foreign word can hope to convey the wealth of connotations produced by the two syllables in Spanish. The classical idea of poetic inspiration, as an impulse of the Muses compelling creation from without, is much too literary; the *Dämonische* perceived by Goethe in the playing of Paganini is closer, but still astray. Lorca quotes Goethe's words to Eckermann: "a mysterious power which everyone feels but no philosopher can explain." The poet attempts to explain in his own lyrical manner this "hidden spirit of suffering Spain" (I: 1067). All over Andalusia, from Jaén to Cadiz, the people use the expression, "Eso tiene duende." It can refer to the singing of a *siguiriya*, to a bullfight, or to any event or moment charged with passion and enveloped in grace. But a distinct quality of *duende* is its association with a dark or negative element: perhaps dissonance in music, a certain darkness in painting, death or tragedy in poetry. Lorca tells us that the famous *cantaor* Manuel Torres once said while listening to Falla play his *Nocturno del Generalife:* "Everything with black sounds has *duende*." The Greco of glowering skies, the Goya of the black murals, and the bloody Christs of Juan de Juni are examples of this strange force in

Spanish art. In poetry, the mysticism of Saint John of the Cross, and Quevedo's obsession with physical decay and death convey the spirit of *duende*.

In fact, *duende* is usually related to death in one way or another. For this reason it has found its most intense expression in Spain, a "country of death" (I: 1073). Only Mexico can be compared to his land, Lorca says. For an alert sensibility, the smallest details of Peninsular life awake secret intimations of mortality: flies, humid cupboards, sand, saints covered with lace, rocks, moss, and thistles. Much of Spanish art revolves around the emotion of death. Among many other examples, Lorca cites his country's tradition of polychromatic sculpture, with its crucifixions and Dolorosas; the Escorial, the painting of Zurbarán, the poetry of Jorge Manrique.

Duende must not be confused with artistic virtue or technical competence, Lorca continues. In fact, they may even be inimical to one another. Mere formal ability is not enough; the catalyst of inspiration is also required. *Duende* is not to be found in the vocal cords of a singer or in the hands of a pianist; its source is much deeper. Its roots sink into the mud from which the first life arose, "in tender intimacy with volcanoes, ants, the wind and the vast night embracing the Milky Way" (I: 1079).

As a power that springs from the depths of the earth, Lorca tells us that *duende* is linked to the dark realm of the unconscious; it is an enemy of reason. It does not descend from Aristotle, but from the Dionysian Greeks, passing through Nietzsche. This demon cannot be summoned at will, but when it arrives its force is irresistible. It shakes the man it possesses like an electric charge.[16]

Lorca makes a perceptive distinction between *duende*—the characteristic form of inspiration in Spain—and the muse of Germany, or the "angel" of Italy. The muse dictates to man, awakening his intelligence and imagination. Unfortunately, these are not the faculties that produce the best art. The muse elevates the poet on a marble throne and garlands his brow with a laurel wreath, but makes him forget the subterranean forces that undermine his seat. For its part, the Italian angel flies over man's head, spilling its grace and light. Man responds with ease, creating forms of beauty and order. In contrast to *duende*, both the German muse and the Italian angel flee from death in horror. The muse "composes an epitaph with a hand of wax" and the angel "weaves an elegy of icy tears and daffodils" (I: 1075). While they flee from death, the Spaniard opens his wounds and revels in his own agony. His inspiration, as we have seen, does not come from outside, but from within himself.

All the arts can express *duende*, but it reveals itself most readily in music, dance, and spoken poetry, since they require live interpretation at a precise juncture of time and space. For the same reason, it finds a wide field in bullfighting. Like the sea and sky in a storm, *duende* cannot repeat itself. It depends on an actual present, being a perpetual baptism of the moment. Its appearance is received with a kind of religious ecstasy. In Arabic music, Lorca tells us that the participants cry "Allah! Allah!"—an exact parallel of the "Viva Dios" of *cante jondo* and the "Olé" of bullfighting. At this hallowed instant, those who are present feel a "communion with God through the five senses" (I: 1072). Something greater and stronger than man has dwelt among them.

As in his analysis of the verse of *cante jondo*, Lorca occasionally seems to be projecting his own poetic ideas and practices onto the subject of his lecture. He tends to praise some of the noble figures of Spanish art in terms of flamenco, which hardly apply in a rigorous sense.[17] Yet beneath the subjectivity and exaggeration lies a remarkable distillation of truths and insights. At times, Lorca's power of perceiving the subtle filaments that unite sensations and objects becomes almost uncanny. His perceptions are not couched in the language of philosophy; in accordance with the spirit of *duende* they are conveyed through image and metaphor, as in poetry. The important point for us is that Lorca selects a word and concept of flamenco—*duende*—as a criterion for judging all works of art. This lecture might be considered a statement of Lorca's esthetics, his ars poetica.

We have seen that *cante jondo*, while it cannot be called pure folk music, has a definite relation to traditional or popular forms of expression. It is worthy of note that a major Spanish poet of the twentieth century, Lorca, has taken a word and idea from the margins of society to measure the spiritual depth of all artistic works. A certain disdain of seriousness and organization informs Lorca's lecture—a preference for instinct over reason, poverty over wealth, individuality over convention. To judge from the testimony of those who knew him, the same qualities seem to have characterized his personality.

Perhaps the poet understood the essence of *duende* because it was the hidden force that animated his own life and art. This inspiration is the indefinable power that makes his poetry compellingly attractive to peasants and literati alike. The phenomenon of Lorca must be understood as the success of an accomplished artist and a magical character.[18] In this sense it was a peculiarly Spanish success, and in keeping with the nature of *duende*. His penchant for reciting his own poetry (he was well known in Madrid before the publication of his first works) and his love of drama, music, bullfighting, and *cante jondo* are aspects of his search for the unique, unrepeatable moment of plenitude. His was a demon of the instant.[19] In contrast to most Western thought from the time of the Greeks— Plato, Christ, Marx—it scorned duration in favor of the present. It only breathed in an atmosphere of tragedy, yet could be playful and ironic in the face of destiny. As we shall see, Lorca's was the voice of one man at a given moment, but it spoke for a whole race and reverberated with the echoes of centuries.

Chapter Two

Practice: Granada, 1922

A history of the Concurso del Cante Jondo, held in Granada in 1922, pertains more to a biography of Lorca than to a study of his works. But before leaving all else behind for the poetry, it would be well to take a brief look at this important event in the modern development of flamenco. It is closely related in time and conception to Lorca's lectures and his *Poema del cante jondo*.

Manuel de Falla seems to have been the motivating force behind the concurso.[1] The composer was deeply concerned about the degeneration of the ancient music of southern Spain. He communicated his concern to the coterie of musicians, writers, and artists that surrounded him in Granada, among them the young Lorca. Falla's preoccupation soon became a program for action: a competition would be organized to create interest in the authentic Andalusian song and to save it from corruption. As usually occurs in these situations, the group's enthusiasm exceeded its economic resources, but the help of the municipal government and the Centro Artístico y Literario of Granada, which sponsored the project, converted Falla's plan into a reality. Lorca gave his first lecture, and a benefit concert was organized in the Hotel Alhambra Palace. Andrés Segovia and Porcel provided guitar music, classical and flamenco; the poet recited from his fresh *Poema del cante jondo*. Other sponsors of the competition included the composers Turina and Oscar Esplá, the musicologist Adolfo Salazar, the painter Zuloaga, the poet Juan Ramón Jiménez, and men of letters like Alfonso Reyes, Ramón Pérez de Ayala, and Fernando de los Ríos.

The event was to be held in the Alhambra during the celebration of Corpus Christi, on June 13 and 14. According to the program, its purpose was to "stimulate a cultivation of the ancient songs in the people, completely forgotten in many places. This competition . . . has as its intention the rebirth, preservation and purification of the ancient *cante jondo*."[2] Only the forms considered to be of antique origin were allowed; above all, the *siguiriya gitana.* Modern, "flamenco" genres were expelled from the outset: *malagueñas, granadinas, sevillanas, peteneras*. Moreover, in accordance with Falla's and Lorca's belief that commercialization was largely responsible for the decadence of this music, only nonprofessional singers were permitted to enter the contest. A jury, presided over by Falla and the old *cantaor* Antonio Chacón, would determine the winners.

It is not hard to conjure up those two evenings on the Alhambra Hill. A group of artists under the direction of Zuloaga had decorated the Plaza de los Algibes for the occasion. This marvelous patio is bounded by the fortress of the Alcazaba, the palace of Charles V, myrtle beds, and the parapets overlooking the Darro gorge and the hill of the Albaicín. The surrounding towers were lit by Bengal lights, which illuminated the rectangle of the little stage and seats below. In a special box sat a group of music critics, in another the Spanish and foreign press. The stage was adorned with blue and white Granadine tiles, hung with native rugs and embroidered *mantones*.

The actual results of the competition—the winners and the losers—are of little interest here, nor were they the chief concern of Falla and Lorca. To a limited extent, the concurso achieved its purpose of revitalizing and purifying the basic forms of *cante jondo*. A few archaic genres that had nearly fallen into oblivion were brought to light, recorded, and in this sense rescued from extinction. The competition or festival of this type became the model for later flamenco activity to which its musical, literary, and discographic flourishing is largely due. The concurso also fulfilled the purpose of rehabilitating *cante jondo* among a limited group of artists and intellectuals. Lorca's generation differed partially from the preceding one in its attitude toward Andalusian music. Raised in a period that associated flamenco with variety shows, dingy taverns, and loose morality, writers like Eugenio Noel, Baroja, and Unamuno naturally despised it. Lorca, Juan Ramón Jiménez, Gerardo Diego, and other younger men, as well as a few foreigners, would perceive the potential beauty of these songs beneath their vulgar exterior. In the past fifty years, few major Spanish creators, from Picasso to Joaquín Rodrigo, have failed to have some kind of contact with flamenco.

In spite of its unique success, the Concurso del Cante Jondo did not quite live up to the hopes it had inspired. This was not necessarily due to the ineptitude of the organizers, but to the nature of the reality they were striving to alter. The live, traditional art of the Andalusian song is a natural enemy of official actions, and the participants in that Granadine nocturne must have seen the event beneath a subtle light of irony. Between them and the sponsors yawned an enormous abyss of background and culture, crossed at most in a few fleeting moments of musical rapture. *Cante jondo* thrives in intimacy, not in public. Its currents flow too deeply to be diverted from above.

Not all of the concurso's limited success can be imputed to the force of circumstance. We have already discussed the fundamental misunderstanding that undermined Falla's—and Lorca's—ideas on *cante jondo*. When it was applied to the organization of the festival the results had to be less than perfect. Falla's prejudice against professionals led him to limit the competition to amateurs; the quality of the performances naturally suffered. This does not mean that there was no fine singing and playing, or that fresh talent was not uncovered. One of the winners was an old man of seventy-three nicknamed "El Viejo," who had walked to Granada from Puente Genil for the contest; he sang variations of *siguiriyas* that made some of the listeners cry.[3] Another old man, Bermúdez, walked all the way from the province of Seville and performed *serranas* as rich in feeling as they were bare in technique. But these men could hardly be expected to reach the level of the great maestros who might have participated: Manuel Torres and Pastora Pavón, for example, to mention only two revered in particular by Lorca. Ironically, the jury's technical advisor was none other than Don Antonio Chacón, the flamenco virtuoso nonpareil. One of the winners of the contest, the young Manuel Ortega, would later become famous as "Manolo Caracol." Ortega did not exactly spring from the grass roots: he belonged to a long line of gypsies in Cadiz who had maintained an almost hieratic musical tradition for generations. The exclusion of professional singers from the concurso naturally lowered the artistic level of the performances. Moreover, this event alone could not wholly stop the vulgarizing trends in *cante jondo*.

The sponsors' criteria were probably too restrictive. Not only did they confine the contest to amateurs. They also limited the musical repertoire to the most "ancient" genres of Andalusian music, which are merely current variants of certain root forms. Two examples are the famous "siguiriyas de Silverio" (Franconetti) and the "malagueñas de (Antonio) Chacón." Falla, Lorca, and their colleagues parted from the belief that *cante jondo* is a more or less static art, whose only hope for survival rests with the primitive forms. More room might have been left for variation within each genre. What matters is the permanence of the type, which can be interpreted in a potentially infinite number of ways. Like all music transmitted orally, flamenco is basically dynamic. It only resorts to old forms when incapable of creating new ones. Just as there are as many ways of executing a *verónica* as there are bullfighters—within the recognized limits of the form—there are as many ways of performing a *siguiriya* as there are singers. The essence of the type must remain intact, but this does not exclude a wide variety of personal interpretation. The performers in the concurso must have felt shackled by the restrictions the jury had imposed: *duende* does not thrive in chains, nor has it ever held rules in high esteem.

Though it would be hard to imagine a more ideal setting for a music festival than the Alhambra, Granada may not have been the best location for the concurso. Falla, a native of Cadiz, was an adopted son of Lorca's city. Like an outsider, the maestro tended to invest Granada with glamour in his writing, and to exaggerate its importance in the development of *cante jondo*. According to him, it was the "chief fire in which the elements that gave birth to the Andalusian dance and song became fused, though special forms and names of these songs and dances were later created in other parts of Andalusia, where they have been better preserved."[4]

Granada was the wrong place to look for the best *cante jondo;* it has never claimed a significant interpreter of the *siguiriya*, for example, the form considered by Falla to be the archetype of the primitive Andalusian song.[5] The genres most typical of the city, the *granadina* and *media granadina*, require great virtuosity in performance, but they produce more admiration than emotion in the listener. With their elaborate trills and ornaments they are examples of the kind of musical decadence that appalled Falla and Lorca, and for this reason they were not allowed to be sung in the concurso. Granada is not part of the zone in southwestern Andalusia that has always been the cradle of flamenco. It has been said that with the exception of the Sacromonte, the soil does not contain the "salt" required for this kind of music.[6] Perhaps Granada is too Moorish, too introspective and refined.[7] Its choice as the location for the festival implied a definite prejudice in its favor; many potential participants must have been unable to travel there.

Yet we still benefit from the concurso; its memory persists as a goal for which to strive, an unexcelled ideal. At no other time has such a cornucopia of artistic talent been gathered together in the cause of *cante jondo*. Falla's ascetic purity, Lorca's inspired fervor, and the self-sacrificing zeal of the other sponsors must have been infectious: they informed, ennobled, and guided the event from beginning to end. It was probably the festival of "greatest artistic transcendence held in Spain in modern times."[8] It laid the cornerstone for the modern rebirth of Andalusian music and it showed the possibilities—and the limits—of enlightened, public influence on a traditional art form. To an extent, the Granadine concurso revealed Lorca's and Falla's lack of theoretical and practical dominion over the facts of Andalusian music. Only in the private, intuitive orb of poetry did Lorca capture the substance of *cante jondo*.

II. Echoes and Motifs

Chapter Three

Echoes: Space, Time, the *Saeta,* Visceral Suffering, Extremes

There are not many direct echoes of *cante jondo* in Lorca's work. The sources of his poetry are hard to trace since he drank from the well of popular inspiration; only rarely did he draw on written materials. When we point out an apparent correspondence between a traditional text and one of Lorca's, we are often merely indicating our own reference and not that of the poet, who probably received his own impetus from a live source.[1]

Most of Lorca's allusions to *cante jondo* occur in his early work. In *Mariana Pineda,* for example, the heroine recites a slightly modified *siguiriya* discussed by the poet in one of his lectures:

> Pues si mi pecho tuviera
> vidrieras de cristal,
> te asomaras y lo vieras
> gotas de sangre llorar.
> [II: 152]

In the original version, called "gypsy and very Andalusian" by Lorca, the first two lines read

> Si mi corazón tuviera
> birieritas de cristar
> . . . .
> [I: 989]

These verses must have seemed too uncultivated for the dignified Mariana. Even in modified form they do not fit her personality, standing out sharply from the rest of her speech. Perhaps Lorca had not yet learned to weave traditional elements into the deeper texture of his work. He had more success in *La zapatera prodigiosa,* where the proletarian origin of the characters lends itself to the employment of popular songs and customs. The shoemaker's wife echoes part of a famous flamenco poem on one occasion, without the disparity of tone we noted in Mariana Pineda: "Mi marido me dejó por culpa de las gentes y ahora me encuentro sola, *sin calor de nadie"* (II: 306).[2]

The *Poema del cante jondo*, though inspired by Andalusian music, contains only a handful of direct allusions. Each of the main divisions of the book is obviously based on a corresponding flamenco genre—*siguiriya gitana, soleá, saeta, petenera*. But Lorca did not attempt to imitate these songs; only rarely does he borrow an individual verse or two. The rather trite second line of "Muerte de la Petenera"—

> En la casa blanca muere
> la perdición de los hombres
> [I: 193]

is a transcription from a well-known song of the same name:

> Quien te puso Petenera
> no te supo poner nombre,
> que debía de haberte puesto
> la perdición de los hombres.[3]

Lorca normally employed a traditional source as a mere point of departure for an original creation. His use of the geographic and temporal precision of popular poetry offers an illustration. The verses of *cante jondo* often describe a definite location in Andalusia:

> Entre Córdoba y Lucena
> hay una laguna clara . . .[4]

Lorca adopted this toponymic technique in his own verse. In the "Escena del teniente coronel de la Guardia Civil," the words of the gypsy speaker might derive from a traditional *copla:*

> Cazorla enseña su torre
> y Benamejí la oculta.
> [I: 226]

Even in the later *Diván del Tamarit*, the poetry reveals a kind of neighborhood pride for Granada, whose spirit is evoked in several lyrics of the book:

> Solamente por oír
> la campana de la Vela
> te puse una corona de verbena.
> [I: 576]

Apparently no one has pointed out the provenance of this refrain. It probably derives from a flamenco poem:

> Quiero vivir en "Graná"
> porque me gusta oir
> la campana de la Vela
> cuando me voy a dormir.[5]

The inclusion of the traditional verse no longer jars our ear since the poet has sewn it into the fabric of his own voice and style.

Just as he employed the geographic precision of popular poetry, so Lorca learned to employ its temporal exactitude. The opening lines of "La casada infiel" in the *Romancero gitano*, for example ("Fue la noche de Santiago / y casi por compromiso"), echo a *siguiriya gitana* of Manuel Torres:

> Era un día señalao
> de Santiago y Santa Ana
> . . . . [6]

In the *Llanto por Ignacio Sánchez Mejías*, Lorca carries to an obsessive extreme this folkloric tendency of designating a specific hour for the action. The whole universe seems to revolve around the fatal hour of the bullfighter's death: "A las cinco de la tarde" (I: 551-52).

The indirect echoes of Andalusian music in Lorca's work are far more pervasive and important than the rare direct allusions. His mind must have teemed with traditional rhythms, melodies, and verses. During the act of creation, they occasionally came to the surface, as we have just seen. More often, they exercised a subtler influence, vaguely molding the poet's expression and even his approach to reality.

The *saeta* or Easter Passion song probably left a greater impact on Lorca's poetry than any other genre of flamenco.[7] Apart from the "Poema de la saeta" in *Poema del cante jondo,* there are traces of this song, its spirit, and the popular customs it represents throughout his work. In his first collection of verse, *Libro de poemas,* some of the imagery—vivid and plastic—already reveals a faint air of *saetas:*

Los Niños
¿Qué tienes en tus manos
de primavera?
Yo
Una rosa de sangre
y una azucena . . .

The dramatic form, the season of spring, the flower symbolism, the blood
and the contrast of colors—white and red—recall the *saeta*. The theme of
this lyric is in fact the poet's debt to traditional music:

Los Niños
¿Quién te enseñó el camino
de los poetas?
Yo
La fuente y el arroyo
de la canción añeja.
[I: 96-97]

In the *Romancero gitano,* the color imagery and the sharp profile of
persons and things reflect the same sensibility. Even where we least expect
them, echoes of the *saeta* fall on our ears. When the lascivious wind chases
the gypsy girl in "Preciosa y el aire," Lorca creates an ironic overtone by
inserting the popular phrase for the approaching Christ in Easter processions: "¡Míralo por dónde viene!" (I: 396). The opening lines of "Muerto
de amor" constitute a variation of numerous *saetas:*

¿Qué es aquello que reluce
por los altos corredores?
[I: 421]

The question-and-answer sequence characterizes many of these Andalusian songs:

¿Qué es aquello que reluce
por cima del Sacramento?
—Será la Virgen María
que va por agua a los cielos.[8]

Lorca's ballad even preserves the form of the response: "Será que la gente
aquella. . . ." The poem acquires its atmosphere of mystery and expectation from the first lines, which resonate with unconscious echoes of the
Passion. The death in this ballad, like the deaths of Christ and so many

Lorcan heroes, evokes the mythic sacrifice of a young god whose blood brings hope for renewal. A final trace of the *saeta* in the *Romancero gitano* has no tragic overtones. The foppish protagonist of "San Gabriel" suggests a kind of mock-heroic Jesus. The poet describes him with the inflated rhetoric of Andalusian songs in the first five verses, which he playfully explodes in the anticlimactic sixth:

> Un bello niño de junco,
> anchos hombros, fino talle,
> piel de nocturna manzana,
> boca triste y ojos grandes,
> nervio de plata caliente,
> ronda la desierta calle.

The laudatory tone of some later lines—

> En la ribera del mar
> no hay palma que se le iguale,
> ni emperador coronado
> ni lucero caminante
> [I: 414]

looks forward to these famous verses of the *Llanto:*

> No hubo príncipe en Sevilla
> que comparársele pueda,
> ni espada como su espada
> ni corazón tan de veras.
> [I: 554]

Within a remarkable range of moods, extending from the burlesque to the profoundly tragic, we perceive the same basic poetic attitude of wonder and praise.

The surrealistic world of Lorca's experimental verse—*Poeta en Nueva York*, the great *Odas* to the Blessed Sacrament and Salvador Dalí—is not as foreign to this atmosphere as we might think. In the horrifying truth of the first work, in its stark objectivity and merciless clarity, Carlos Ramos-Gil has glimpsed another reflection of the esthetic that we have seen in the *Poema del cante jondo*, the *Romancero*, and the *Llanto*. Like the *saetero*, Lorca "seems to feel and enjoy poetically the naked horror of death, of pure death. . . ."[9] In the "Oda al Santísimo Sacramento del Altar," the vast imagery of sin and redemption condenses in the small, tangible wafer of the Eucharist (I: 763-73). The divinity becomes incarnate in the Host, a "little tambourine of flour," as in the wooden images of Andalusian Easter processions. In fact Lorca's Christ resembles that of the *saeta:* "not a rigid and distant effigy to whom a prayer could hardly reach, not an incomprehensible dogma nor an abstract and inoperative article of faith, but a definite, present figure, near the senses . . . limited in form and time . . . concrete, approachable, nameable, undeniably real, as when He roamed the earth."[10] In his poetry Lorca surrounds religion with the variegated scenery of a supreme drama. The Christian dimension of his work can be found in this exaltation of the Baroque imagery so characteristic of Andalusian churches, processions, and the *saeta.* Significantly, Lorca dedicated his ode to Manuel de Falla, who had stimulated his interest in *cante jondo.*

Some critics have even found the model for Lorca's popular style in the *saeta.*[11] This is no doubt an exaggeration; the poet's interpretation of traditional verse surpassed by far the narrow scope of any particular form. *Cante jondo* represented only one aspect of his lifelong dedication to Spanish folklore. Nevertheless, we have seen how the *saeta* left many traces on his work, from beginning to end. He never imitated these religious songs, but absorbed and sublimated their lyrical essence, using their phrasing and ecstatic tone to convey personal emotions and themes. Sometimes he evoked the *saeta* in order to awaken ironic overtones. Finally, his approach to religion, immediate and concrete, had much in common with the climate of this song. After all, the *saeta* and his poetry are two supreme expressions of the Andalusian sensibility.

Just as religious emotion is revealed concretely in *cante jondo,* other feelings tend to manifest themselves in a physical form. For this reason, tears, blood, and corporal suffering appear constantly, as in Lorca's first lecture and in this example:

> Has 'e bení a buscarme
> con el corasón partío,
> yorando gotas de sangre.[12]

In the following *martinete,* the lover's anguish and memory of past happiness are symbolized by his burning intestines, yellow hot as in a forge:

> Así como está la fragua,
> "jecha" candela de oro,

> se me ponen las entrañas
> cuando te recuerdo, y lloro.[13]

The two examples, which could be multiplied almost indefinitely, are representative of traditional Andalusian verse. First, the emotion becomes so intense that it manifests itself in the body: blood, tears, intestines. Second, love causes the unbearable pain. Third, there is a carnal or even visceral quality in this pain.

In contrast to other lyric poets of his generation—Juan Ramón Jiménez, Jorge Guillén, Pedro Salinas—Lorca usually did not directly bare his personal feelings in his verse. His poetry has an unmistakably objective and collective bias. The soul that uncovers itself in the *Romancero gitano*, for example, does not belong to him alone, but to a whole people—the gypsies, Andalusians, Spaniards, and by extension, all men.[14] For this reason, we do not find many verses similar to the above two songs in Lorca's major poetry. In the lyrical passages of his mature drama, on the other hand, the characters are not so reluctant to expose their feelings.

Bodas de sangre demands our attention above all, since it is the most Andalusian and folkloric of Lorca's plays. Its basic element is a deep passion that burns inside the characters and drives them to their tragic end. This passion finds release in concrete images and in transpositions from the affective to the physical world. Between the Novia and Leonardo especially, we sense an almost palpable current of desire mingled with hate. After their flight together from the wedding feast she cries to him:

> ¡Ay, qué lamento, qué fuego
> me sube por la cabeza!
> [II: 600]

He then describes the futility of his former attempts to suppress his love for her:

> Con alfileres de plata
> mi sangre se puso negra,
> y el sueño me fue llenando
> las carnes de mala hierba.
> [II: 601]

In the final scene, the mother of the dead bridegroom says that her tears will not come from her eyes, but from the soles of her feet, from her very roots: "Vuestras lágrimas son lágrimas de los ojos nada más, y las mías vendrán cuando yo esté sola, de las plantas de los pies, de mis raíces, y serán más ardientes que la sangre" (II: 610).

In *Yerma*, Lorca continued to use the same kind of imagery. The protagonist's maternal urge and a certain visceral quality recall the feminine characters of Unamuno. A whole constellation of related images surrounds Yerma: flesh, bowels, teeth, bones, veins, milk, blood. She muses to herself on one occasion:

> Estos dos manantiales que yo tengo
> de leche tibia son en la espesura
> de mi carne dos pulsos de caballo
> que hacen latir la rama de mi angustia.
>
> [II: 662]

Compared to her, the heroine of *Doña Rosita la Soltera* seems to lack substance. Yet she also reveals her emotions in objective, anatomical images:

> Tierna gacela imprudente
> alcé los ojos, te vi
> y en mi corazón sentí
> agujas estremecidas
> que me están abriendo heridas
> rojas como el alhelí.
>
> [II: 719-20]

In *La casa de Bernada Alba,* Lorca's last play, he returns to the frustrated and erotic realm of *Bodas de sangre;* the youngest daughter, Adela, reminds us of the Novia. She says of Pepe el Romano, her secret lover: "Mirando sus ojos me parece que bebo su sangre lentamente" (II: 832).

As in this passage, the majority of the above examples—from both Lorca and *cante jondo*—revolve around an image of blood. Usually it symbolizes sexual desire. In the wedding song of Andalusian gypsies, known as the *alboreá,* blood evokes the ritual proof of the bride's virginity:

> Jesucristo te llama
> desde su huerto,
> coronadito de espinas
> y el pelo suelto.
>
> En un verde prado
> tendí un pañuelo;

> salieron tres rosas
> como tres luceros.[15]

In this marvelous interplay of images, Christ's blood, sacrifice, and innocence foreshadow the role of the bride, who is about to enter into the Christian sacrament of marriage. Lorca obviously had the *alboreá* in mind when he wrote *Bodas de sangre*. The Novia's loosened hair, indicative of her new life, appears in the wedding song:

> Despierte la novia
> la mañana de la boda
> . . . .
> Que despierte
> con el largo pelo
> . . . .
> [II: 560-61]

Some later verses contain the motif of marriage and blood, set against a rural background that vaguely recalls the *Song of Songs:*

> Porque el novio es un palomo
> con todo el pecho de brasa
> y espera el campo el rumor
> de la sangre derramada.
> [II: 570]

As the very title of the play suggests, blood is its central symbol. In Lorca's work, the most meaningful events of human life—love, marriage, death—imply a shedding of the sacred fluid. As in the poetry of *cante jondo,* blood fulfills a complex role. It may represent a mere chromatic touch; more frequently it suggests sexual desire or death. Occasionally it acquires metaphysical attributes, as in the second part of the *Llanto* and in the *saeta*.

Blood symbolism represents only one aspect of the visceral suffering we have observed in flamenco verse and in Lorca's drama. The point is not to prove that Lorca imitated the traditional songs of Andalusia, but to understand how he absorbed them into his own lyrical world.[16]

The revelation of emotional suffering through corporal images could be considered another facet of Lorca's extremism—a quality of his work discussed by many critics. Anguish becomes so unbearable that it seeks expression in the most severe kind of pain—physical pain. In Lorca's great tragedies, we watch the characters struggle with their feelings, which are too strong to be repressed. Finally these burst forth in all their nakedness as if still connected to the speakers' nerve endings. Since emotions are so powerful, language must be pushed to its metaphorical limits in order to convey them.

In his first lecture on *cante jondo,* Lorca asserts that the poetry of this music lacks a middle tone. Love and death constitute the two basic poles; they leave little room for the development of intermediate themes. "The Andalusian either cries to the stars or kisses the reddish dust of his roads." The deepest forms of this music flourish only in extreme states—religious or sensual ecstasy, freedom, death, guilt. The poems do not usually describe or comment on these states. Their involvement is too direct to permit the luxury of moral or philosophical speculation.

Even more than *cante jondo,* Lorca's poetry could be said to lack a middle tone. It oscillates between the two extremes of love and death, plenitude and tragedy. But the dark hemisphere of his work casts a long shadow over the realm of light. Nearly half of the lyrics in the *Poema del cante jondo* contain variations on the theme of death.[17] In the *Romancero gitano,* ten ballads deal with death or its approach, only two with fulfillment; the three poems on the patron saints of Andalusian cities are playful and festive. The *Poeta en Nueva York* reeks with mortal blood, and the *Llanto* might be considered a modern version of the medieval Triumph of Death. In other words, the great majority of Lorca's work revolves around extreme situations. An intermediate world does exist, but to a limited extent, consisting of trees, flowers, plants, animals, and the generic characters who form a kind of chorus in the background of the main action. Young girls, for example, do not have an individual countenance or personality; by the very fact of their age and sex they will normally be sensual and frustrated. The mothers will be sad and resigned to suffering, the lot of all Lorcan women. On the other hand, the principal characters possess a clear profile and individuality. Between them we do not witness a subtle exchange of influence and feeling. Their contacts resemble the collision of planets, as in "La casada infiel" or "Thamar y Amnón." Love is reduced to its lowest common denominator, sex, and to its crudest form, rape. "The equipoise between lover and beloved, so fundamental in our refined notion of this passion, is quite absent from the gypsies of Lorca's *Romancero,* the beloved being nothing more than the object on which the sexual violence of the lover is spent."[18] Other human relations are also reduced to a level of primitive violence. When Lorca leaves this climate of intensity, as in the nostalgic lyrics of his youth, his verse loses force and interest. Like *cante jondo,* his poetry thrives in a climate of extremes.

In contrast to other poets, Lorca did not attempt to reproduce the verse of the Andalusian song. We should recall the words of his first lecture, where he warns against a servile imitation of folk poetry. The most talented exponent of the tendency criticized by Lorca was probably Manuel Machado, who may have had a better theoretical and practical grasp of flamenco than any other modern poet. His *Cante hondo* (1912) constituted an early step in the literary renaissance of this music. But Machado, in contrast to his wiser brother Antonio, squandered much of his creative energy in efforts to reproduce popular lyrics. The fact that some of his verses have become part of the flamenco repertoire attests to his "success." Yet these poems have a merely local appeal, with no impact outside of Spain. Machado failed to elevate the Andalusian song to a superior artistic plane, or to reveal its ancient, mythic roots. This is what Lorca achieved, though he knew less than other poets about the technical facets of *cante jondo.*

Chapter Four

Motifs and Themes

In addition to the direct and indirect echoes of *cante jondo* in Lorca's work, there are several common motifs and themes in these two expressions of Spanish art. The most important of these include *pena negra*, the peculiarly Andalusian sense of suffering; the guitar, characteristic instrument of flamenco and a neglected motif in Lorca's poetry; and the bull and bullfighting, which are closely related to the world of *cante jondo* in Spanish life.

PENA NEGRA

We have seen that *duende*, the muse of flamenco and to a certain extent of Lorca too, thrives under duress. It reveals itself musically in dissonance, or "black sounds," and in a sense of pain, anguish, and frustration—*pena* or *pena negra*. This feeling is so vast and deep that it escapes words; it condenses in the cry of the *siguiriya gitana* or Lorca's *Poema del cante jondo:* "¡Ay!" The motives of this pain cannot be enumerated or defined with precision. Language, whether in the lyrics of songs or the words of poetry, merely provides a guidepost. These motives find their only adequate expression in music; the poet's problem is to translate the feeling to another medium.

   In the verses of flamenco songs, *pena* sometimes appears as an immediate sentiment, occasioned by the death of the mother or the beloved, by an amorous failure, by loneliness. If it were not for the strength of the music the words would remain lifeless and empty. Poets like Manuel Machado have attempted to discover the motives of *pena*. The feeling loses its power when reduced to specific causes:

> Madre, pena, suerte, pena, madre, muerte;
> ojos negros, negros, y negra la suerte.[1]

Lorca goes beyond these incidental factors to the substrate from which *pena* arises and the sediment it leaves in man. For him, this feeling is more than a human reaction to a given event: it is a whole atmosphere, a vital and lyrical climate.

Like the emotions we saw in the previous chapter, *pena* also materializes in a concrete form through the verses of Andalusian music. Here are two examples:

> Yo quise pesá mis penas,
> pero ya no puo ser;
> por más que yo la buscaba
> la pesiya no encontré.

> En la soledá der campo
> me puse a yorar mis penas,
> y fue tan grande mi llanto
> que florecieron las yerbas.[2]

This emotion receives its maximum expression in the verses of the *siguiriya gitana*, which sings of "pains without possible consolation, wounds that will never close, crimes without human redemption . . . the lament of the earth that will never be the sky, the sea that knows no limits, the goodbye forever, eternal."[3] As the name of the song suggests, the opening cry and the threnody of its melody seem to evoke the millennial sadness of the gypsies, their resignation or despair in the face of suffering.

In Lorca's *Poema del cante jondo, pena* is both a human cry and a vague, impersonal exhalation of the earth:

> Tierra
> vieja
> del candil
> y la pena.
> [I: 167]

The singers of *saetas* come to Seville during Holy Week from remote countries of suffering:

> Vienen de los remotos
> países de la pena.
> [I: 179]

Like *duende*, its inspiration, *pena* springs directly from the soil. Perhaps it would be more precise to say that *pena* is in the soil. For this reason, it cannot be transformed into a mere human feeling, hence its hopelessness.

Lorca said of his *Romancero gitano* that its only real character is *pena* itself (I: 1084).[4] Indeed, the same might be said of nearly all his Andalusian poetry. One ballad in the *Romancero*—the "Romance de la pena negra"—especially develops this theme. It is important for understanding Lorca's approach to Andalusia, the gypsies, and *pena*.

> Las piquetas de los gallos
> cavan buscando la aurora,
> cuando por el monte oscuro
> baja Soledad Montoya.
> Cobre amarillo, su carne,
> huele a caballo y a sombra.
> Yunques ahumados sus pechos,
> gimen canciones redondas.
> Soledad, ¿por quién preguntas
> sin compaña y a estas horas?
> Pregunte por quien pregunte,
> dime: ¿a ti qué se te importa?
> Vengo a buscar lo que busco,
> mi alegría y mi persona.
> Soledad de mis pesares,
> caballo que se desboca,
> al fin encuentra la mar
> y se lo tragan las olas.
> No me recuerdes el mar,
> que la pena negra, brota
> en las tierras de aceituna
> bajo el rumor de las hojas.
> ¡Soledad, qué pena tienes!
> ¡Qué pena tan lastimosa!
> Lloras zumo de limón
> agrio de espera y de boca.
> ¡Qué pena tan grande! Corro
> mi casa como una loca,
> mis dos trenzas por el suelo,
> de la cocina a la alcoba.
> ¡Qué pena! Me estoy poniendo
> de azabache, carne y ropa.
> ¡Ay mis camisas de hilo!
> ¡Ay mis muslos de amapola!
> Soledad: lava tu cuerpo
> con agua de las alondras,
> y deja tu corazón
> en paz, Soledad Montoya.

Por abajo canta el río:
volante de cielo y hojas.
Con flores de calabaza,
la nueva luz se corona.
¡Oh pena de los gitanos!
¡Oh pena de cauce oculto
y madrugada remota!
[I: 408-09]

In his first lecture, Lorca described the personification of *pena* in *cante jondo:* "it becomes flesh, takes on human form and acquires a definite line. It is a dark woman who wants to catch birds with nets of wind" (I: 987). He has obviously used a similar personification in this ballad. As in the verses of flamenco, anguish is felt so intensely that it becomes material, filtering through Soledad's body, blackening her skin and clothes, boring through them like a parasite. In fact, Soledad is *pena negra* incarnated. The repetition of her name, and of the word *pena* itself, produces the incantatory effect of music in the poem.

The action occurs at dawn, the hour of passage, of transition, of death, and the most characteristic hour in Lorca's verse. Another topos is the bitterness of despair expressed in the lemon juice of Soledad's tears:

Lloras zumo de limón
agrio de espera y de boca.

The characteristic color of this ballad, apart from the blackness of pain, is a kind of golden yellow. We note the yellowish copper of the woman's complexion, her thighs like poppies, the dry leaves, the lemons, the pumpkin flowers. Everything seems to discharge a bittersweet quality of ripeness and age. Is it the protagonist's age, that of the gypsies, or that of the sad and suffering earth? At any rate, *pena* is old, as old as human feeling. It may be related to emotions like despair or guilt. In Soledad we sense an unsatisfied sexuality in the visceral imagery associated with her and she is tortured by memories of the past, but we could not say that desire or remorse are the causes of her anguish. *Pena* does not have causes, because it is timeless and thus without beginning or end. The patterns of imagery that vertebrate the "Romance de la pena negra," and the sublimation of an anecdotal emotion into a mysterious lyrical ambience, demonstrate how Lorca transforms a traditional theme into a universal poetic expression.

Lorca once said that *pena* is a more celestial than earthly feeling (I: 1084). In this sense it could be seen as a yearning for the infinite in a world limited by matter. *Pena* is not action, but an expectation that will never be fulfilled. It is black because it is hopeless. It is the anguish of being and of nothingness.

Through the magic of word and rhythm, through an intuition of the hidden roots of suffering in his people, Lorca transposed to the medium of poetry what had only been expressed before in music.

THE GUITAR

It would be surprising if Lorca had not shown a predilection for the guitar in his life and work: the instrument plays an essential role in the world of *cante jondo*. We may recall the poet's comments in his last lecture on the ancient Andalusian song, where he revealed a perfect understanding of the guitarist's function (I: 998-99). His enchantment with the instrument might be said to have obeyed a racial and family inclination. One of his father's ancestors, a certain Frasquito García, was a professional guitarist who emigrated to Paris, married, and died there.[5] Lorca's father had the custom of organizing flamenco sessions at his son's natal house in Fuentevaqueros, near Granada. The poet inevitably found a guitar in his lap at an early age and even took some lessons from an aunt.[6] They did not last long, since he turned to a serious study of the piano. But as late as his stay in New York, he apparently still "played the guitar with great verve and spontaneity."[7]

As we might expect, the guitar is a recurrent motif in Lorca's work. Its music forms part of the background for his youthful prose descriptions and dramas; in one of his volumes of verse, the *Poema del cante jondo,* the instrument constitutes a luminous symbol. In Lorca's later books, the guitar appears less frequently, like all of the typical and somewhat picturesque elements of his native Andalusia, yet it left an undying echo in his ear.

Two mentions of the guitar in Lorca's first published works may give us a key to the instrument's function in his lyrical world. Both relate to the Albaicín, the gypsy quarter of Granada. Lorca depicts the city in a poetic evocation of color and sound with distant music of "sorrowful guitars" suggesting "cries of love and passion" (I: 883, 931). These two aspects of the instrument—its association with love and with sorrow—flow like a pair of rivulets from a common stream throughout Lorca's writings. The negative aspect prevails in his first book of verse, *Libro de poemas*. In "Elegía," he invokes the Andalusian girl who is the poem's subject:

> Venus del mantón de Manila que sabe
> del vino de Málaga y de la guitarra.
> [I: 40]

The Malagan wine could be a kind of muscatel. It probably relates to the sweetness of desire, though its saccharine taste leaves a slightly bitter or medicinal residue on the palate—like everything in Málaga for Lorca.[8] The guitar may stand for the wholly unfruitful side of love and desire which are naturally frustrated in this unlucky sister of Doña Rosita la Soltera and other Lorcan women. I favor such an interpretation because this part of the poem consists of verses built on contrast. ("¡Oh mujer potente de ébano y nardo! . . . ¡Oh cisne moreno! . . .") But the two images, Malagan wine and guitar, are characteristically ambiguous and rich in their possible connotations; Lorca's imagery rarely fits into a tidy scheme.

In two other poems of this volume, the lyre takes the place of the guitar. (All of the popular stringed instruments seem to have approximately the same meaning for Lorca.) The lyre appears alongside of pain in the tenderly Franciscan "Canto de la miel," where it suggests the poet's office and the sorrow of past suffering:

> Para el que lleva la pena y la lira,
> eres sol que ilumina el camino.
> [I: 38]

Finally, in "Invocación al laurel," the lyre and the traditional rose of romantic love point to death:

> Las rosas estaban soñando en la lira . . .
> Conozco la lira que presientes, rosa;
> formé su cordaje con mi vida muerta.
> [I: 135-36]

Three separate lyrics treat the guitar more extensively in the *Poema del cante jondo*. The first, "La guitarra," appears toward the beginning of

the "Poema de la siguiriya gitana," immediately after the presentation of
the scenery for the drama to follow.

> Empieza el llanto
> de la guitarra.
> Se rompen las copas
> de la madrugada.
> Empieza el llanto
> de la guitarra.
> Es inútil callarla.
> Es imposible
> callarla.
> Llora monótona
> como llora el agua,
> como llora el viento
> sobre la nevada.
> Es imposible
> callarla.
> Llora por cosas
> lejanas.
> Arena del Sur caliente
> que pide camelias blancas.
> Llora flecha sin blanco,
> la tarde sin mañana,
> y el primer pájaro muerto
> sobre la rama.
> ¡Oh guitarra!
> Corazón malherido
> por cinco espadas.
>   [I: 158]

The position of this poem at the beginning of the book is very proper,
since the first timid strummings of the guitar usually create the atmosphere
for the performance of *cante jondo,* enticing and drawing the initial notes
from the singer. Moreover, the Lorcan hour of dawn is highly ap-
propriate, time of the classic *fiesta flamenca.* The opening lines, with their
weeping lament, remind us of the *siguiriya* being evoked in this section of
the book. This genre is the most funereal in all *cante jondo.* The language
of the poem approaches the vagueness and the ephemeral quality of music,
especially of music for the guitar. The strong pattern of assonance (*a a*),
the refrainlike repetitions, and the parallel constructions imitate a
monotonous drone:

Es inútil callarla.
Es imposible
callarla.
Llora monótona
como llora el agua . . .

The cups that held the dawn have broken, spilling a wan light and recalling the libations that accompany the flamenco ritual. The guitar's lament can no sooner be silenced than the crying of suffering mankind of which it forms the eternal burden. It wails like running water or the wind that blows across snowcapped mountains, perhaps awakening memories of the Granadine Sierra Nevada. The motive for this wailing lies in a futile yearning for what cannot be: the yearning of hot southern sand for flowers and fertility;[9] of an aimless existence for a purpose and a new life; of a dead ideal for the innocence of a pristine illusion. The poem ends with an image of the guitar as a heart being wounded by the five "swords" of the player's fingers. This image probably refers to the guitarist's right hand in the execution of the *rasgueado,* the characteristic technique of this music. But it also suggests the hearts of Spanish Mater Dolorosas, pierced with knives or swords.

In a brief fragment of the "Gráfico de la Petenera," the focus changes from the musician's fingers to the six strings of the guitar ("Las seis cuerdas"):

La guitarra,
hace llorar a los sueños.
El sollozo de las almas
perdidas,
se escapa por su boca
redonda.
Y como la tarántula
teje una gran estrella
para cazar suspiros,
que flotan en su negro
aljibe de madera.
[I: 191]

The first two lines describe the melancholy beauty of the guitar. The instrument has a special power of awakening the intimate chords that sleep in the memory and unconscious. To fully understand this little piece we have to place it within the framework of the larger composition to which it pertains. The "lost souls" whose sobs escape through the guitar's sound hole belong to the hundred black horsemen, victims of their love for La Petenera. Like a tarantula, the guitar weaves a web "in order to trap sighs," expressing human sorrow through music. These sighs "float" inside the instrument's body as if it were a wooden cistern; the *Poema del cante jondo* is full of foreboding wells and cisterns. In a later poem of the same work we encounter a related image:

> Pasan caballos negros
> y gente siniestra
> por los hondos caminos
> de la guitarra.
>
> [I: 211]

The black horses look back to the dark riders of the poem on the *petenera*, and the "deep roads of the guitar," to the cistern—two indications of the profundity of the instrument's sound. In these and other places of the work, Lorca seems to be portraying the climate of vice that formed a real part of the Andalusian demimonde at the turn of the century, with its seedy taverns and *cafés chantants*. Indeed, the whole "Gráfico de la Petenera" depicts this kind of milieu. It is Lorca's most "antiflamenco" poem.

The final lyric on the guitar in this book is one of the "Seis Caprichos" toward the end of the volume, entitled "Adivinanza de la guitarra." These fragmentary little sketches, with their concision and subtle metaphors, occasionally resemble Oriental verse. Lorca dedicated the entire series to the guitarist Regino Sainz de la Maza.[10]

> En la redonda
> encrucijada,
> seis doncellas
> bailan.
> Tres de carne
> y tres de plata.
> Los sueños de ayer las buscan,
> pero las tiene abrazadas
> un Polifemo de oro.
> ¡La guitarra!
>
> [I: 217]

The poet has suggested the mysterious appeal of the guitar in a few brief lines. The sound hole represents a crossroads where six maidens dance, three of flesh—the treble strings of catgut—and three of silver—the basses. In a poem above we saw how the guitar "makes dreams cry"; here the "dreams of yesterday" search for the dancing maidens. But they are held in captivity by a "golden Polyphemus"—the wooden body of the guitar with its single round eye. The imagery is very accurate: the color of most flamenco guitars in fact approaches a golden hue, owing to the polished cypress used in their construction. Moreover, the dancing maidens, crossroads, dreams, and frustration are echoes of earlier themes in the *Poema del cante jondo.* The Cyclops vaguely evokes the Sicilian cave from the episode in the *Odyssey,* which would be consistent with the deep hollow of the guitar's body. The music of this instrument, with its intrinsically sad sound, seems to have opened secret chambers of the spirit for Lorca. Stirring the turbid waters of the unconscious, it brings to light hidden dreams, memories, and illusions.

The guitar appears incidentally in a few other lyrics of this work. It is an instrument of mourning in "Barrio de Córdoba," where a young girl has apparently died of love (I: 212).[11] Once more in the "Gráfico de la Petenera," Lorca personifies death in a white *vihuela*—an ancestor of the Spanish guitar:

> Por un camino va
> la muerte, coronada,
> de azahares marchitos.
> Canta y canta
> una canción
> en su vihuela blanca,
> y canta y canta y canta.
> [I: 196]

Perhaps the use of the *vihuela* in place of a guitar evokes the *petenera*'s archaic flavor, and its association with the medieval Spain of Christians, Arabs, and Jews.[12] With her withered crown of orange blossoms and her sterile white instrument, the figure of death evokes grotesque visions similar to those of the late Goya.[13] The guitar is also connected with death in another poem, "Memento." The lyric speaker, probably a gypsy, asks to be buried with his guitar:

> Cuando yo me muera,
> enterradme con mi guitarra
> bajo la arena.[14]
>
> [I: 208]

This last will and testament reflects the gypsies' veneration for music as well as a racial custom. Jean-Paul Clébert says that this people used to place stringed instruments in the arms of their dead.[15]

In the *Romancero gitano,* Lorca attempted to purge his work of the picturesque Andalusian objects that fill his earlier poetry. The guitar suffers the same fate as oil lamps, weather vanes, wayside crosses, and street lanterns. It would never again be as important in Lorca's work. Yet strangely enough, he resurrected his favorite instrument in the *Poeta en Nueva York* and in his mature drama. In the volume of verse, the guitar, *vihuela,* lyre, and mandolin provide a melancholy refrain to mortality and suffering. As in the poem on the *petenera,* death, wearing a huge Africa mask, plays a *vihuela.* The mandolin is associated with a dissected frog, the lyre appears in a poem about a Jewish cemetery and the guitar in a climate of radical loneliness, anguish, and despair (I: 471, 504, 520, 547).

In most of Lorca's plays, the music of these instruments forms a kind of counterpoint to the usually tragic action. As in the poetry, their presence may prelude love, death, or suffering. In the dramas of Lorca's last years, the guitar acquires a new modality. The sinuous shape of its wooden body suggested a woman's figure to the poet, as it had to many other artists before. In the rather experimental *Así que pasen cinco años,* the guitar is a symbol of the passionate "Novia":

Creo que me vas a quebrar entre tus brazos, porque soy débil, porque soy pequeña, porque soy como la escarcha, porque soy como una diminuta guitarra quemada por el sol. . .

[II: 396]

Background music on the instrument has the effect of an aphrodisiac on the feminine protagonist of *Amor de Don Perlimplín con Belisa en su jardín,* and in *Yerma,* a similar music accompanies the fertility dance of the devil and his wife (II: 333, 687). In *Doña Rosita la soltera o El lenguaje de las flores,* the lute, a new member of Lorca's family of stringed instruments, is a correlative of the heroine's body. Rosita says to her boyfriend in the first act:

¡ . . . rompes con tu cruel ausencia
las cuerdas de mi laúd!

[II: 719]

Though Lorca's plays and poems are full of direct allusions to the
guitar, these do not exhaust its importance in his work. The instrument
may function as an image or symbol with a definite meaning, but it exer-
cises a more pervasive and subtle influence in the rhythms, tones, and dynamics of Lorca's verse. The *Poema del cante jondo,* in particular, has
been interpreted by some critics as a lyrical fusion of poetry and music for
the guitar. The verse incarnates the land from which traditional Andalusian songs derive, the human feelings they express, and their musical substance—of which the guitar is a fundamental element. Ángel del Río has
noted that music and poetry at times merge so completely that the resulting
sensation can only be translated by "imagining the deep plucking of a
guitar's bass strings":[16]

> Tierra seca,
> tierra quieta
> de noches
> inmensas
> . . . .
> Tierra
> vieja
> del candil
> y la pena.
> Tierra
> de las hondas cisternas.
>
> [I: 167]

Christoph Eich has gone even further in his comparison between this
volume and the sound of the guitar. He believes the poems represent a
pure transformation of the instrument's music into words, manifested in
dynamic variations from *piano* to *forte,* in the delicate shadings of tone
color, and in the richness of rhythms and pauses.[17] According to Gustavo
Correa, the rhythmic feeling of the *Poema del cante jondo* could be interpreted as the modulation of a human cry accompanied by the vibration of
the guitar. A kind of lyrical tension would be the primary structural principle of the work, revealing itself in the human voice, in the pulsations of the
guitar's strings, and in images of trembling, wavering, and undulation.[18]

The intimate tone of the *Poema del cante jondo* penetrates our ear with the subtlety and intimacy of music for the guitar. In the *Romancero gitano,* music condenses into color and form, while the tone becomes more objective. In the *Llanto por Ignacio Sánchez Mejías,* Lorca also goes beyond the small, private world of flamenco and the guitar, yet the poem may have been modeled on the gypsy lament.[19] Its scope and structure are closer to a symphonic or choral composition than to music for a solo instrument, but the guitar is not entirely absent. Its music forms the burden to the death and tragedy of the work, much as in Lorca's plays. After the bullfighter's goring,

> Comenzaron los sones del bordón
> a las cinco de la tarde.
>   [I: 551]

The changes in tempo and intensity in the poem recall the guitar's variations in rhythm, tone color, and dynamics. In the second part, for example, the movement of the verse becomes more and more urgent until it is cut by a sharp "No" of the refrain, in the manner of a guitar whose strings are suddenly dampened by the player's right hand:[20]

> ¡Oh blanco muro de España!
> ¡Oh negro toro de pena!
> ¡Oh sangre dura de Ignacio!
> ¡Oh ruiseñor de sus venas!
> No.
> ¡Que no quiero verla!
>   [I: 555]

It is not easy to summarize the meaning of the guitar in Lorca's poetic world. A son of the last years of the nineteenth century, he inherited the tradition of what Marcel Raymond has called the "guitars of elegiac romanticism."[21] The instrument's music formed a plaintive and superfluous background to some of his youthful prose and drama, but the poet soon transformed this stale tradition into a completely personal and modern myth. The guitar remained in association with love, but not with the nostalgic romance of the past. Perhaps because of its shape, he began to relate it to woman's body and sexual desire. Desire is rarely fulfilled in Lorca's work and the guitar came to suggest the frustration of love, and a consequent suffering and pain. In the hard wood of its sinuous form he seemed to glimpse the limits of human yearning:

> Sueño concreto y sin norte
> de madera de guitarra.
> [I: 437]

In his brief article on Regino Sainz de la Maza, Lorca characterized this guitarist as being essentially melancholy. "Melancholy, like the man who wants to fly and realizes he is wearing iron shoes; melancholy, like the man who goes hopefully to a witch's grotto and finds it decorated with English furniture; melancholy, like all of us who cannot display the splendid wings that God has placed on our shoulders" (I: 1119). This was also the quality Lorca divined in the guitar and the one he incorporated in his own work. It is not entirely foreign to the feeling of *pena negra.*

Just as the lyre was the emblem of ancient poetry, the guitar might have been Lorca's. In some of his verse the instrument seems to incarnate the lot of the poet, who sheds more tears than ordinary men:[22] he bears the weight of all human suffering in order to purify and sublimate it through art. Few instruments can express the "black sounds" of anguish and despair as well as the guitar. In his only composition for the instrument, Manuel de Falla interprets the dark spirit of *cante jondo* through the sonorities and dissonances of the impressionist composers.[23] In Lorca's poetry, the black sounds of Andalusian music have their equivalent in recurrent omens and somber presences: the moon, wind, sand, horsemen, unlucky colors.

The guitar could also be compared to the poet's muse insofar as it represents a fusion of popular and artistic traditions. For several hundred years it has been the instrument of the people in Spain.[24] But as early as the sixteenth century, one of its ancestors, the *vihuela,* had become well known in aristocratic circles. Composers began to write variations on popular songs in an elegant style. "The melodies forged by the people, unpolished and full of passion, are carried by the *vihuelistas* to the Court, where they acquire the delicate amatory accent that characterizes them" (I: 1120). Lorca would do something similar in his adaptations of folk songs, though he considered himself to be a mere collector. In our century the guitar has enjoyed another renaissance. Composers such as Turina, Villa-Lobos, and Rodrigo have written pieces for it in a contemporary idiom without abandoning a popular inspiration. Lorca's own poetry represents a marvelous union of traditional forms and motifs with the most modern technical resources and a unique sensibility.

How could we fail to sense a profound correspondence between the poet's art—receptacle of a live tradition—and the guitar, in which the essential values of former instruments have concentrated without a loss of its own unique character? This character it owes to the people. The guitar's intimacy naturally attracted Lorca's poetic ear as perhaps another expression of the miniaturist's art so typical of Granada.[25] Another Granadine, a friend and contemporary of Lorca, has been almost wholly responsible for the instrument's modern revival. I am of course referring to Andrés Segovia. The grace and depth of his musicianship have much in common with the poet's muse, yet the flamenco guitar probably offers a closer parallel with Lorca's poetry. Here the player does not seek precision or sweetness of tone. Everything—technique, rhythm, melody, harmony—is subordinated to a superior force, which might be called intensity. Or in the language of the Andalusian, *duende*. As in Lorca's work, the power of feeling seems to overflow the boundaries of form. The flamenco guitarist strains at the limits of consonance while Lorca goes beyond the verge of meaning, each creating an atmosphere of strange beauty, foreboding, and despair.

THE BULL AND BULLFIGHTING

As we might expect, bulls and bullfighting constitute recurring themes in Lorca's poetry. As his generation reevaluated Andalusian music, it also restored the national *fiesta* to an honorable place in Spanish culture. Lorca said that bullfighting is probably the "greatest poetic and human treasure of Spain, incredibly unexploited by writers and artists, due mainly to a false pedagogic education we have received and which the men of our generation have been the first to reject. I think bullfighting is the most cultured pastime in the world today; it is pure drama, in which the Spaniard spills his best tears and his best gall. It is the only place where one can go and with certainty see death surrounded by the most astonishing beauty" (II: 1023-24).

Bullfighting and *cante jondo* form an esthetic whole in Andalusian life. The two activities are conjoined by subtle, ancient ties. The terminology of one has passed to the other: we hear of a *cantaor* singing *por naturales* for example. The *natural*, the simplest and perhaps the most difficult pass with the *muleta* in bullfighting, is used figuratively in this expression to indicate an extremely pure style of singing. Some critics believe there may be a common cultural heritage behind the two arts. Perhaps the dominant role played by the gypsy in both would explain the apparent kinship. This people is probably of Indian origin, as we have seen. *Cante jondo* shows definite Oriental traits; bullfighting evokes the ancient Eastern worship of the bull as a source of strength and fertility. Walter Starkie has called this common heritage the "Mithraic mystery, with its infinite ramifications and its bonds of interest."[26] The lover of flamenco is often an *aficionado* of the bulls. These endeavors have in common a rhythmic nature, spontaneity, and a special communion between the artist and his public. All of these qualities tend to produce *duende*.

The themes of bulls and bullfighting occur chiefly in Lorca's mature work, especially in the *Romancero gitano* and, of course, the *Llanto por Ignacio Sánchez Mejías*.[27] In the first ballad of Antoñito el Camborio, we see the handsome, spruce young gypsy on his way to a *corrida* in Seville:

> Antonio Torres Heredia,
> hijo y nieto de Camborios,
> con una vara de mimbre
> va a Sevilla a ver los toros.
> [I: 417]

These verses echo the opening lines of a famous Salamancan folk song harmonized by Lorca:

> Los mozos de Monleón
> se fueron a arar temprano,
> para ir a la corrida
> . . . .
> [I: 796]

For the Spaniards who know the bloody outcome of the popular song, the mere mention of Antoñito's going to a bullfight casts an ominous shadow over the poem. In addition, the bulls of the initial lines establish a pattern of imagery that runs throughout the two ballads. Antoñito is jailed by the Guardia Civil before he reaches Seville, and the *corrida* he will never see is projected onto the natural scenery, in accordance with his fertile imagination:

El día se va despacio,
la tarde colgada a un hombro,
dando una larga torera
sobre el mar y los arroyos.
[I: 417]

The fading day slowly disappears with the "afternoon hanging from its shoulder," in the manner of a bullfighter performing a pass in which the cape is elegantly draped from the shoulder with one hand. The taurine imagery continues in the second ballad when Antoñito is stabbed to death by his four cousins:

Cuando las estrellas clavan
rejones al agua gris,
cuando los erales sueñan
verónicas de alhelí
. . . .
[I: 419]

As López-Morillas points out in his article on the *Romancero,* the first image of these verses is an example of how Lorca represents the "willful violence of inanimate things."[28] Nature asserts herself in a clash of elements in his poetry, and often transmits her frenzy to men. In this sense, Antoñito el Camborio's death is a reflection of the cruel violence of nature embodied in an image from the world of bullfighting.

Lorca's treatment of the bull reaches a climax in the *Llanto* (I: 549-58). In the first part of the poem, we see the concrete bull of the arena once again, in this case the historic quadruped that mortally gored Lorca's friend. But as the work progresses, this bull evolves into a much more important animal: the mythological bull of Mediterranean cultures, a symbolic figure united to mysterious images and possessed of a terrible power. From the real animal in the ring, we advance to the bulls of Guisando, silent and sphinxlike, "casi muerte y casi piedra," then to "celestial bulls" and taurine ghosts in search of redeeming blood. Finally, Lorca presents a lucid, climactic image: against the white wall of Spain, a black bull of pain and suffering.

¡Oh blanco muro de España!
¡Oh negro toro de pena!

This metaphor may derive from *cante jondo*, in which the bull sometimes stands for *pena*. The following is a *siguiriya gitana:*

> Encerraíto me veo
> en mi soledad
> con el torito de mi pena negra
> que me va a matar.[29]

The bull represents a complex symbol in Lorca's verse. In most of the *Llanto* it seems to incarnate the forces of darkness. It is the instrument of Sánchez Mejías' tragic end, even threatens the man's peace after death: the poet hopes the cadaver will not be disturbed by the "double panting of bulls." In the *Romancero gitano,* the bull also accompanies death. It embodies the strife of "Reyerta"—

> El toro de la reyerta
> se sube por las paredes
> [I: 398]

and the dramatic bellow of the "bull of anvils" preludes the violence of "Martirio de Santa Olalla" (I: 433). Yet in certain parts of the *Llanto*, the bull seems to be more a passive element than an active instrument of fate or death. In fact, the animal may be subject to these very forces. The ancient bulls of Guisando bellow with the weight of centuries on their backs, weary of treading the earth. In a related and even more pathetic image, the "cow of the old world" appears with its bloody snout and sad tongue:

> La vaca del viejo mundo
> pasaba su triste lengua
> sobre un hocico de sangres
> derramadas en la arena
> . . . .

The action of the *Llanto por Ignacio Sánchez Mejías* could be seen as a ritual sacrifice. The poet was well aware of the *corrida*'s religious aspect. In one of his lectures he mentions the "liturgy of bullfighting, an authentic religious drama where a God is worshiped and sacrificed, in the same way as in the Mass" (I: 1077). All nature converges at the appointed hour in the *Llanto* to witness the ceremonial spilling of blood. Ignacio mounts the stands of the ring as a sacrificial victim would climb the steps of a temple; a "thirsy multitude" observes the solemn event.

> Por las gradas sube Ignacio
> con toda su muerte a cuestas.

Buscaba el amanecer,
y el amanecer no era.
Busca su perfil seguro,
y el sueño lo desorienta.
Buscaba su hermoso cuerpo
y encontró su sangre abierta.
¡No me digáis que la vea!
No quiero sentir el chorro
cada vez con menos fuerza;
ese chorro que ilumina
los tendidos y se vuelca
sobre la pana y el cuero
de muchedumbre sedienta.

The destinies of the bull and the matador are bound together; Ignacio resembles a "dark minotaur" in death. The animal embodies a supreme force of the earth, and the man acquires some of its strength in the rite on the sand. Ignacio and the bull are united by their common shedding of blood.

Because of its power, size, and beauty, the bull was often considered an incarnation of the life-force in ancient religions. Its sacrifice, with the flowing of blood, was believed to fecundate the earth. Lorca remained faithful to the tradition of his land in his treatment of the bull; perhaps the oldest cult in Andalusia is that of this animal. It has been "sacred among the Hispanic people since the times of Gerion."[30] Other poets of Lorca's generation also dealt with the bull in their work: Rafael Alberti, Gerardo Diego, and Fernando Villalón. They treated the animal principally in the context of the *corrida*. Notwithstanding the quality of their taurine poetry, it lacks the depth and mystery of Lorca's. The Granadine poet was not chiefly concerned with bullfighting as a spectacle, but with the sediment of symbolism and myth that underlies its colorful exterior.

Thus the bull appears surrounded by a luminous transcendency in Lorca's poetry, evoking its primitive worship as a divine figure. One critic has suggested that the bull embodies fate in the *Llanto:* "a totemic animal immolated in a close struggle with the man who performs the sacrifice. . . ."[31] This seems to be corroborated by the animal's eventual identification with another Lorcan divinity—the moon—also connected with fate. The sacrifice in the *Llanto por Ignacio Sánchez Mejías* occurs beneath an ominous lunar brilliance:

> Dile a la luna que venga,
> que no quiero ver la sangre
> de Ignacio sobre la arena.

The crescent shape of the bull's horns suggests the moon to the poet's imagination: "que finge cuando niña doliente res inmóvil." The fusion of bull and moon is not a Lorcan invention; they have been associated with each other since ancient times. Just as the moon presides over the death of the characters in *Poema del cante jondo* and *Romancero gitano,* it illumines the scene of Ignacio's death with a fatal glow. In Lorca's exaltation of these two archetypal symbols, bull and moon, we begin to perceive the mythic dimension of his poetry.

III. Lorca, *Cante Jondo,* and Myth

Chapter Five

The Mythic Land: Andalusia

Few poets have been more rooted in their native soil than García Lorca. From it he drew his nourishment and his inspiration. "I love the earth," he said; "I feel myself joined to it in all my emotions. My most distant memories of childhood have a taste of the earth" (II: 958). In Lorca's work, Andalusia is more than a mere theme or lyrical background. Often it constitutes the very marrow of his poetry. It is the touchstone of his career, his *querencia:* the place to which he always went back for vital and artistic regeneration. The *querencia* is the place to which a fighting bull instinctively tends to wander in the ring; there he is most confident and formidable. "During Lorca's sojourns abroad, or in Madrid, he always returned for poetical strength to his native province; even when he did not return to it in person, he returned in imagination, memory, and dreams: and it never failed him as a source of strength and inspiration."[1] One of the reasons for his limited success in translation is precisely this closeness to the roots of his land. Lorca's work abounds in local elements. When the original spell of language disappears, his work tends to lose some of its power, which seems to spring from the soil of his native province.

The lyrical settings of *cante jondo* and Lorca's poetry have much in common. Both represent an Andalusia inspired by the concrete area of southern Spain, yet far removed from the real world of parallels and meridians. Lorca mentions the nocturnal atmosphere of the primitive Andalusian song in his first lecture; his own poetry also belongs to that realm of darkness. The tutelary goddess in both cases is the moon. In the same lecture Lorca discusses the "pantheism" of *cante jondo*. "All exterior objects acquire a definite personality and shape until they take an active part in the lyrical action" (I: 987). In much of his own work we breathe the same air, inanimate things are vivified, and human life may become inert. In the *Poema del cante jondo,* the characters appear as lifeless effigies against a hostile background; the wind, olive trees, cactus, and agaves have the capacity for movement and feeling. In this work, the *Romancero gitano* and the *Llanto por Ignacio Sánchez Mejías,* natural objects possess helpful, or more commonly, harmful powers. The wind forebodes an approaching tragedy, a stagnant pond clamors for a victim, the moon heralds the arrival of death. Man forms part of the physical world and natural phenomena are represented in human terms. This double impulse, dehumanizing on the one hand and anthropomorphic on the other, is a constant in Lorca's poetry and *cante jondo.* We seem to be in a primitive, mythic world in which man is still an integral part of nature and the cosmos. It is significant that in the poet's non-Andalusian verse, where he is farthest from his native land and the spirit of flamenco, this interaction between man and his surroundings is not operative. Gustavo Correa has called the *Poeta en Nueva York* an "anti-mythic" work.[2] In Lorca's previous volumes, man is always threatened by misfortune, but his life and even his death achieve plenitude within a universal order. In the poems based on his stay in the United States, man is divorced from nature with its rhythms of cyclic renewal.

In addition to this primitive atmosphere of his Andalusian poetry, Lorca's treatment of his native region embodies a kind of personal myth. As we will see, his vision of this land descends in part from the Arabs, but his lyrical Andalusia does not correspond to any previous treatment in verse or prose. It transcends all possible sources. This poetic land has two poles: the interior and the coast, symbolized in turn by the olive and the sea. The interior or hinterland, with its dry, parched earth, is the birthplace of tragedy and *pena negra.* It is also the breeding ground of the deepest and best *cante jondo.* The coast, with its changing mosaic of the sea, is a less fateful land, though not untouched by the shadows of suffering and death. Within the interior region, Granada and Cordova stand out in sharp relief. Seville is the capital of the seaboard region. In Lorca's mythic Andalusia these cities are both a lyrical setting and the protagonists in a struggle of cosmic dimensions between past and present, heaven and earth.

A POETIC TRAJECTORY

Perhaps the best gauge of the importance of flamenco elements in a given Lorcan work is the presence or absence of Andalusia. The two themes are so bound together as to be almost inseparable. They resemble a pair of overlapping threads in a tapestry, always bearing a direct relation to each other. We remember that *cante jondo* and its inspiration, *duende,* are intimately connected to the earth.

In Lorca's youthful *Libro de poemas* (1921) and *Primeras canciones* (1922), few of the lyrics give a precise impression of Andalusia, so striking in the later works. His *Canciones,* whose composition more or less parallels the *Poema del cante jondo* (1921-1924), introduce the theme of three cities: Granada, Cordova, and Seville (I: 305-17). In this order of importance they recur throughout his work. His natural preference lay with Granada, of course, but Cordova was also close to his sensibility. Long past their primes of splendor, Moorish or Roman, the melancholy and solitude of these two cities awakened a special sympathy in the poet. Seville, with the exception of her *saetas,* was probably too powerful and optimistic to engage his intimate affection. Lorca was a true Andalusian— he could plunge into the Sevillian "bacchanal of flesh and laughter";[3] but this aspect of his personality manifested itself in his life more than in his writing.

The poet finally discovered the lyric potential of his native land and found his own voice in the *Poema del cante jondo*. The Andalusia he portrays here does not correspond exactly to reality, nor even to the countryside depicted in the verses of the region's traditional songs. As we might expect, the work unfolds in a nocturnal atmosphere, or in the dubious light of dawn, the coldest and the cruelest hour, the hour of death and tragedy. I do not know a more lightless volume of poems than this. The sun never appears. At most, the twilight of dawn suggests its approach and the moon reigns in the sky, spilling an ominous, greenish light over the land. The towns in these poems are only illuminated by the wan flicker of oil lamps and street lanterns.

The inevitable triad of Andalusian capitals occupies a central place in the *Poema del cante jondo*. Very few other cities appear. The crux of this book consists of four poems corresponding to the *siguiriya gitana*, the *soleá*, the *saeta*, and the *petenera*. The *saeta* constitutes a separate island in this Lorcan geography, since it belongs to Seville alone. To a lesser extent, the *petenera* pertains to Cordova. The other two pieces are more rural than urban, and also more generic. Just as the *siguiriya* and the *soleá* are the basic forms of Andalusian music, they are the most profound and representative parts of this work.

The two poems present a dry and ancient land with a low sky and dark horizon (I: 155-76). It seems to be made up of a flat expanse, almost a desert, interspersed with occasional hills and mountains. In the latter live gypsy cave dwellers. The dryness of the region is revealed by its white dust, lime, slow-running water and deep cisterns. A mysterious wind blows across it stirring the dust and bearing strange premonitions. This is chiefly an uninhabited country with a few small towns. These have narrow streets and alleys, whitewashed houses with balconies and weather vanes, churches with towers, crosses, and tolling bells. The flora of the landscape consists of ubiquitous, centenary olive trees, symbols of age; cypresses, with their shady memories of death and graveyards; orange trees, whose golden fruits conceal an acid pulp, like the leaves of the oleander. Cactus and agaves complete the vegetation, partly Mediterranean and partly African. The fauna is even more forbidding than the land: dark birds, enormous flies, sleepy horses, and black butterflies.

The first section of "Poema de la soleá" offers a concentrated picture of Lorca's mythic Andalusia:

> Tierra seca,
> tierra quieta
> de noches
> inmensas.
>
> (Viento en el olivar
> viento en la sierra.)
>
> Tierra
> vieja
> del candil
> y la pena.
> Tierra
> de las hondas cisternas.
> Tierra
> de la muerte sin ojos
> y las flechas.
>
> (Viento por los caminos.
> Brisa en las alamedas.)

It goes almost without saying that the scene is nocturnal. The wind over the parched land forebodes the tragedy to follow; it is the only sign of life or movement. The lantern sheds a pale light of impending violence. (In a later poem dedicated to the street lantern, the round eyes of a dead gypsy shine in its flickering light [I: 218].) The stagnant wells also prelude death, a dark anonymous end. Besides the impersonal wind, the real protagonist of this poem is the pain of the nameless men who inhabit the land and the sadness of the ancient earth.

This Lorcan geography does not refer to a specific location. The landscape of the *Poema del cante jondo* could be seen as a poetic representation of the anguish expressed in traditional Andalusian music. Yet if we were forced to locate this lyrical country we would have to choose upper or interior Andalusia, in particular the provinces of Granada and Cordova. They contain the kind of land symbolically depicted by Lorca, with their lonely plains and mountains, far from the sea and the gaiety of Seville, Málaga, and Cadiz. They embody what the poet calls the "Andalucía del llanto," where the earth seems to groan under an Oriental curse, and human activity is consumed by a timeless inertia (I: 168).

Humans in fact play a secondary role in these poems. They appear for a brief moment, then fade into the impersonal, primordial world of matter from which they seem to spring. Christoph Eich has said that the *Poema del cante jondo* represents a world at the beginning of creation.[4] Space and time exist, but without form or duration. All action condenses into its minimum expression: floating, trembling, wavering. Human activity is reduced to its lowest common denominator—a cry or a scream, the flash of a knife blade in the darkness. The mysterious beings who populate these verses barely stand out against the physical background; the women dress in mourning, the men shroud themselves in capes. As in *cante jondo*, the most common colors are black and red, but Lorca diffuses them in a vague sfumato. If his landscape looks back to Genesis, it also anticipates the Apocalypse. Perhaps the deathly riders and the horizon "bitten by fires" recall the medieval paintings that portray the Triumph of Death and the Last Judgment. As usual, Lorca is the poet of extremes.

There are some pertinent similarities between this work and José Ortega y Gasset's essay, "Teoría de Andalucía." Ortega seems to formulate some of Lorca's poetic intuitions in more rational terms. According to the philosopher, we must remember the antiquity of Andalusia if we wish to understand its culture—one older than the Greek or Roman. This culture is essentially rural. Ortega does not say this in a pejorative sense; he is referring to the intimate connection between the people and their soil and sky. In contrast to the Castilian or Catalonian, for example, the Andalusian does not seek to modify the external world. He is basically passive to his surroundings, like a plant; unlike other men, he does not strive to mold the environment to his desires. Ortega calls this outlook on life the "vegetative ideal." The clemency of the weather and the fertility of the soil enable the Andalusian to subsist with a minimum output of energy. His proverbial laziness should not be considered a simple weakness or vice; the vegetative ideal does not represent a finality in itself. It is a means to an end, a way of escaping the routine and concentrating on what is essential—namely, the very act of living life in its purest, existential expression. Ortega recalls Schlegel's remark that indolence is the last remnant of the earthly Paradise, and he says Andalusian culture is the only one in the West which remains faithful to a paradisiac ideal of life. These people live submerged in their surroundings like plants or flowers. They place the land above themselves in order of importance as if they were no more than beneficiaries of its boundless wealth. The union of man with the earth is not merely a physical fact for them, but a spiritual relationship, an ideal that has almost become a myth.[5]

Ortega could have read Lorca's *Poema del cante jondo* when he wrote his essay, but aside from the remarkable similarities, some basic differences characterize the two works. Lorca's mythic Andalusia is also an unmistakably ancient land. Its culture appears to be chiefly rural, and his characters barely react upon their environment. In their intimacy with the earth, they resemble plants or even more, stones. The important distinction is this: for Ortega, the Castilian outsider, the Andalusian's vegetative existence has a positive value; for Lorca, who knew it from the inside, it bears a negative sign. For the philosopher, it represents a path to personal fulfillment and wisdom; for the poet, a curse and the inertia which must be overcome in order to achieve freedom and plenitude. Ortega saw the pleasant side of Andalusia: the sunshine, the sea, the abundance of the soil with its olives, grapes, and oranges. His mental image corresponds to lower maritime Andalusia—the plain of the Guadalquivir, Cadiz, and Málaga, the city where he spent part of his youth. Lorca's landscape, the land that "sighs for the sea," cannot be pinpointed on a map, being a poetic representation of the interior area of his native region. If Ortega's Andalusia is an earthly paradise, Lorca's more closely recalls a living hell.

In the *Romancero gitano*, written between 1924 and 1927, Lorca's Andalusian poetry reached its summit. The poet himself called his *Romancero* "antiflamenco." "It is the poem of Andalusia," he said, "and I call it gypsy because the gypsy embodies what is most elevated, profound and aristocratic in my country, and what is most representative of its manner. . . . A book where the Andalusia we see is hardly expressed'' (I: 1084). Indeed, these ballads evoke a fantastic world of mountains and plains, horsemen and olive groves, towers and corridors. This is the atmosphere of the "Romance sonámbulo," for example, perhaps the most typical of the work. This atmosphere does not exactly parallel that of the *Poema del cante jondo*. It is tragic and nocturnal, but also more variegated and humanized. In the earlier book, human activity resembles at most the momentary flash of a knife blade. Here it resembles a brilliant radiance. Like the rose colored clouds of a sunset, it must lose the battle against the night, but for the observer it is triumphant.

The three great cities of southern Spain also hold a place of honor in the *Romancero*. We see the melancholy of Granada, the loneliness of Cordova, and the brilliance of Seville. One ballad, the "Romance de la pena negra," seems to evoke the mythic land of the *Poema del cante jondo* (I: 408-09). As we have seen before, the action occurs at the crucial Lorcan hour of dawn. In the dialogue with an imaginary interlocutor that constitutes the central part of the poem, Soledad Montoya says:

> No me recuerdes el mar,
> que la pena negra, brota
> en las tierras de aceituna
> bajo el rumor de las hojas.

Pena negra does not belong to the open world of the sea, but to the lonely interior, the land of olive groves and the rustle of dry leaves. We are in the world of *cante jondo* once again.

Certain elements in other ballads also recall this climate: the cistern and the agaves in the "Romance sonámbulo," the whitewashed façades and the street lamps in "Muerto de amor," the oleander and dark mountains in the "Romance del Emplazado," and above all, the nominally Palestinian landscape in "Thamar y Amnón," with its dry wind and scorched, waterless earth (I:400-03,421-22,423-25). Nevertheless, the light, color, and vitality of these poems separate them from the gray, monotonous world of the *Poema del cante jondo*. The latter represents a lyrical projection of Andalusian music. The *Romancero gitano* is much more than this: a fusion of the regional with the universal, an almost inevitable law of great Spanish literature.

The surrealistic atmosphere of the *Poeta en Nueva York* (1929-1930) and the two odes—to Salvador Dalí and the Blessed Sacrament—are not as foreign to Lorca's Andalusian world as might be expected. However, this matter lies outside my study.[6] The poetry of Lorca's last years, on the other hand, concerns us directly. These years were marked by a return to the old *querencia*—Andalusian music and folklore. This is the period of the *Llanto por Ignacio Sánchez Mejías, Diván del Tamarit* (1934-1935), and the folk tragedies. "So Lorca comes full circle to the starting point of his first works. In *Bodas de sangre*, in *Yerma,* in the *Llanto*. . . .we find ourselves in the same human climate, elemental and passionate, of the *Poema del cante jondo* and the *Romancero gitano.* A return to the world of Andalusia. Now, in a splendid plenitude, the accessory and the picturesque are suppressed—only essences count."[7]

As the critics have pointed out, the *Llanto* contains a mixture of the regional style of Lorca's Andalusian poetry and the symbolic manner of the *Poeta en Nueva York* (I:549-58). He has placed the scenery of the early works in a more universal framework, and he has purified it. There is a notable absence of the quaint oil lamps, street lanterns, and flowering balconies that occasionally clutter the *Poema del cante jondo* and to a lesser extent, the *Romancero gitano.* If he sang to the accompaniment of the guitar before, he orchestrates a complete symphony now. The landscape of the *Llanto* is definitely Andalusian, but it differs in subtle ways from the lyrical setting of the previous books. The bullfighter's goring and agony take place in an urban atmosphere; this dissolves into a mysterious rural climate in the remainder of the poem. Though it does not refer to the real world, this climate shows certain resemblances to lower Andalusia. Not to the grace and luminosity of Seville, but rather to the Guadalquivir basin with its swamps and plains. Lorca portrays a damp, rocky, end-of-the-world country, bathed in the moon's cold splendor or enveloped in fog. The dominant color is gray: "y la plaza gris del sueño." Everything is shrouded in a strange mist. The poet recalls his dead friend's valor with the "last *banderillas* of gloom"; the bullfighter's symbolic blood goes singing over marshes and meadows, "wavering soulless in the fog." Secret voices come from the ranches, shouting to "celestial bulls": "mayorales de pálida niebla." To describe his friend's physical annihilation, Lorca imagines gray rain that splatters as it falls on stones, the same stones that crush skeletons of larks and "wolves of penumbra." The poet asks for a river of "sweet mists" to carry Ignacio's body to the sea. Autumn will come with its "grapes of mist."

As in the *Poema del cante jondo*, all objects lose their form in the last part of the *Llanto*. Men and objects are swallowed in this humid, diffuse world full of fog, rain, and snow, covered by rocks, swamps, moss, grass, willows, cypresses, and olive trees. Ignacio "sought for the dawn," but finds only death. He sought for his confident profile, instead he enters an endless sleep. His body, lying in state, fades into a haze; since it is in decay, nobody will recognize the dead man's former self. But the poet will sing of his grace and figure for posterity, in order that his memory may live on. In the *Poema del cante jondo* we saw how human effort is obliterated by time and decay, the forces that destroy civilizations. In the *Llanto*, man's bravery and intelligence resist being absorbed by nothingness. Death is transformed into art. The death of Sánchez Mejías lies at the opposite pole of the earlier work. It is a death of light, in contrast to the dark, blind end of the anonymous characters in the *Poema del cante jondo*.

SEA AND OLIVE

In the "Romance de la pena negra," we saw the difference between the Andalusia of the sea and that of the interior, the "lands of the olive." We recall that the protagonist of the ballad, Soledad Montoya, asks her imaginary interlocutor not to remind her of the sea. In her state of anguish the mention of the sea would probably bring memories of former happiness; nothing is more unbearable than the recollection of past joy when hope for recovering it has vanished. In a sonnet in honor of Falla that has recently come to light, written about the time of the *Romancero gitano,* Lorca uses similar imagery to express the polarity between the two Andalusias:

> Ocho provincias de la Andalucía
> olivo al aire y a la mar los remos,
> cantan, Manuel de Falla, tu alegría.[8]

And in a later sonnet dedicated to the composer Albéniz, the poet symbolizes the two areas in the "salt of Cadiz" and the waters of Granada:

> Desde la sal de Cádiz a Granada,
> que erige en agua su perpetuo muro,
> en caballo andaluz de acento duro
> tu sombra gime por la luz dorada.
> [I: 700]

But it is in the opening poem of the earlier *Poema del cante jondo,* "Baladilla de los tres ríos," that Lorca develops most systematically his personal vision of two Andalusias. Since the whole book deals with the poet's native land, the first piece—a kind of prologue—introduces the physical background much as the initial stage directions of a play describe the setting for the action. The three rivers in the poem are the Guadalquivir of Seville, and the Darro and Genil of Granada. Just as Cadiz represents lower, maritime Andalusia in the sonnet to Albéniz, so here does Seville. Again, Granada embodies the hinterland.

> El río Guadalquivir
> va entre naranjos y olivos.
> Los dos ríos de Granada
> bajan de la nieve al trigo.
>
> ¡Ay, amor
> que se fue y no vino!
>
> El río Guadalquivir
> tiene las barbas granates.
> Los dos ríos de Granada,
> uno llanto y otro sangre.
>
> ¡Ay, amor
> que se fue por el aire!
>
> Para los barcos de vela
> Sevilla tiene un camino;
> por el agua de Granada
> sólo reman los suspiros.
>
> ¡Ay, amor
> que se fue y no vino!
>
> Guadalquivir, alta torre
> y viento en los naranjales.
> Darro y Genil, torrecillas
> muertas sobre los estanques.
>
> ¡Ay, amor
> que se fue por el aire!
>
> ¡Quién dirá que el agua lleva
> un fuego fatuo de gritos!
>
> ¡Ay, amor
> que se fue y no vino!

Lleva azahar, lleva olivas,
Andalucía, a tus mares.

¡Ay, amor
que se fue por el aire!
[I: 153-54]

Perhaps the best way to reveal the structure of this poem is to make a catalogue of its two major constellations of images, one referring to Seville and the Guadalquivir, the other to Granada, the Darro, and the Genil. This lyric is a modern example of the parallel construction analyzed in earlier Spanish poets by Dámaso Alonso.

Seville	*Granada*
naranjos	nieve
olivos	trigo
barcos	suspiros
alta torre	torrecillas muertas
viento	estanques
azahar, olivas, mares	fuego fatuo de gritos

When it reaches Seville, the Gualdalquivir meanders through groves of orange and olive trees. Oranges, in their shape and color, represent a kind of materialized sun, which contrasts with the snow of the colder, shadier Granada. The olive trees in this case do not symbolize the sadness of the hinterland, as in the "Romance de la pena negra," but suggest the material wealth of Seville and lower Andalusia. Olives inevitably accompany the endless libations of wine in that great city. They form a virtual staple of the Sevillian's diet, much as wheat for the inhabitants of the Granadine *vega*. The fact that *olivos* and *trigo* assonate in Lorca's poem further emphasizes the contrast. Continuing down the list, the objective sailboats on the Guadalquivir become mere sighs on the Darro and Genil. The proud, high tower of the Giralda in Seville stands against the "dead little towers" of Granada—the Alhambra and Generalife—which evoke a bygone glory. The air in Seville is clean due to a wind from the river and sea; the stagnant pools in Granada lie unruffled by a breeze. Finally, down the Guadalquivir flow the products of the economic and spiritual abundance of Seville—olives and orange blossoms. The Darro and Genil bear only a "will-o'-the-wisp" of tragic cries.

In summary, Seville asserts herself in the world with grace and confidence; Granada has its back to reality and the present, enveloped in reveries. Seville is an open city with a beneficent climate; her river leads to the sea. Granada is closed upon itself and has much harsher weather due to the influence of the Sierra Nevada. Its two little rivers do not constitute great avenues to the ocean and the Americas, only cold trickles of melted snow. Seville is brash and extrovert, the city of adventure and intrique, rhythm and dance. Granada loves privacy and is quiet, contemplative, intellectual. "It renounces adventure, travel, exterior curiosities. . . . It despises all this and adorns its garden. . . . Granada is like a story of what already happened in Seville" (I: 939-40). This contrast is partially expressed in the two refrains of the "Baladilla":

> ¡Ay, amor
> que se fue y no vino!
>
> ¡Ay, amor
> que se fue por el aire!

A love affair in Seville, with its real history of abandonment and betrayal, becomes a mere dream in Granada, vanishing into thin air. All that the two have in common is a similar destiny: in both cities, love ends in sorrow. The two Andalusias, upper and lower, Arab and Phoenician, reveal their sorrow in the same kind of song in which the human voice approaches a scream or cry, condensed in the "Ay" of the refrain.

We might ask ourselves what relation Lorca's personal myth of the two Andalusias bears to the area where *cante jondo* flourishes. A hypothetic triangle drawn between Jerez de la Frontera, Morón de la Frontera, and Ronda, has traditionally been called the matrix or cradle of flamenco. Others place this generative zone on an axis between Seville and Cadiz, passing through Jerez.[9] Despite these differences, nearly everyone agrees that the important area is centered in southwestern Andalusia. Surrounding it, a secondary zone can be distinguished which has undergone the influence of the first: the greater part of the provinces of Cordova, Málaga, and Huelva, and the northern part of Seville province. Here, many songs have been developed to a high level of artistry, but they have rarely been indigenous to these areas, not deriving from the matrix or cradle. Finally, the provinces of Granada, Jaén, Almería, and Murcia compose a peripheral zone. Here, the traditional music gravitates toward the Levant, as in the *fandango* and its variants, as well as toward western Andalusia.

Thus Lorca did not live in the real heart of the flamenco country, nor does it occupy the main place in his work. We already know that he felt a greater affinity for Granada and Cordova than for Seville and the coastal provinces. We also remember how he and Falla exaggerated the importance of Granada in the development of the ancient Andalusian song. But the matter is not as simple as it might seem. Though the creative zone of *cante jondo* is located in lower Andalusia, its actual center does not lie on the coast. Jerez, Morón, and Ronda, the three corners of the imaginary triangle, are of course interior cities. Seville, though connected to the sea, expresses itself through dark *saetas* as well as tripping *sevillanas*. With the exception of the *alegrías* of Cadiz and the songs of Málaga, the verses of Andalusian music rarely describe the seaboard. All of the forms considered by Lorca and Falla to be ancient and authentic belong to the interior—the *siguiriya gitana*, the *soleá*, the *serrana*, the *saeta*. On the other hand, many of those they considered to be modern and derivative thrive on the coast—*alegrías, jaleos, guajiras, malagueñas*.

Thus the interior, mythic Andalusia that holds the central place in Lorca's poetry does not correspond to the nucleus of the flamenco country in southern Spain. Yet the two regions—one poetic, the other real—are both removed from the sea. The poet's Andalusia does not represent an area on the map; it is a lyrical condensation of the feelings expressed in *cante jondo*. The pain, loneliness, and suffering that exude from these songs do not harmonize with the brilliant, ever-changing mosaic of the sea. This is music of the "lands of the olive," scorched by the sun or washed in the sterile light of the moon. Lorca himself seems to have lived and felt the contrast between the freedom and optimism of the sea and the hopeless monotony of the hinterland. In a letter to a Granadine friend, unpublished until quite recently, he says: "I really envy you by the seashore. Unfortunately for me my father is an excessive lover of the mountains, and doesn't like to spend much time next to the waves, but for me there is no greater pleasure in life than the contemplation and enjoyment of that gay mystery."[10] Thus the sea haunts the mind of Soledad Montoya, and Bernarda Alba's crazy mother, a prisoner in her daughter's house, cries "to the seashore, to the seashore!" (II: 820). It might be said that Lorca's mythic Andalusia represents the yearning of the interior for the sea. In this respect, his symbolism grew out of conventional Romantic usage, in which the desert or hinterland often signifies spiritual death, and the sea, life and freedom.[11] Yet Lorca differs from the Romantics in the power and complexity of his expression. The two Andalusias, coast and interior, were not literary symbols divorced from his own existence: they embodied a personal vision and an intensely lived experience.

A LORCAN GEOGRAPHY

We have seen in one place or another how the poet characterizes the three major cities that appear in his work. It only remains to see how his characterizations relate to the various forms and genres of *cante jondo*. In addition, I will show briefly how Lorca depicts some other cities in his mythic Andalusia.

GRANADA

Granada was more than a mere city for Lorca. It gave him his blood and his roots and constituted "one of the reasons for his being, the atmosphere and environment without which he could not have lived."[12] We have already looked at his treatment of the city in some detail, but one aspect has not come to our attention: its collective esthetic. "Granada loves what is diminutive," are Lorca's initial and significant words in a lyrical piece of prose (I: 936). He goes on to say that the genuine esthetic of Granada is that of small things, as exemplified by the private gardens and delicate chambers of the Alhambra. The most authentic artistic schools of the city have been composed of miniaturists, from the Moorish architects and masons who fashioned their arabesques in stucco to the Baroque poets, like Soto de Rojas, who wrote in well-turned verses studded with fine images.

We have already had occasion to glance at the flamenco forms common to Granada—the *granadina* and *media granadina*. These may be considered as two more typical expressions of the city's art. Compared to the *siguiriya* or *soleá*, they are miniature songs: in scope and intensity, *cante chico*. They represent the local versions of the *fandango,* the most patently Arabic of all flamenco genres.[13] The *media granadina* in particular seems to reproduce the intricate stuccowork of domes and ceilings in Moorish palaces. To a lesser extent, the *granadina* is an "arabesque of filigrees, in which melisma abounds so much that it damages the purity of the song, like blood that has suddenly been flooded by red globules, which corrupt and destroy it."[14] Even the verses of these songs occasionally seem to disclose a miniaturist's art, as in this *granadina:*

Una crú yevas al pecho,
engarsá en oro y marfí.
Déjame resarle a eya
o crucifícame ayí.[15]

How could we fail to distinguish another manifestation of the Granadine esthetic in Lorca's poetry? Throughout his career he preferred the short lyric and only conceived more ambitious works on a few occasions. He sought concentrated moments of intensity in his poetry, true to the demands of *duende*. In his first collection of verse, he affected a kind of Lilliputian minuteness and Franciscan intimacy: poems to insects, animals, and children. The *Poema del cante jondo* is composed of fragmentary pieces, like far-off snatches of guitar music. In the "Andaluzas" of *Canciones,* he evokes the Arabic spirit of Granada, employing short verses punctuated with diminutives. Here an image of refined synesthesia portrays the silence of the night interrupted by the croaking of frogs:

El silencio mordido
por las ranas, semeja
una gasa pintada
con lunaritos verdes.
[I:312]

The ballads of the *Romancero gitano,* with their chiseled images and brilliant colors, have been called "little pictures drawn in ice by a refined savage."[16] One of these, "San Miguel," ironically depicts Granada and its peculiar art. In a parody of the popular legend, this saint of a church in the Albaicín appears as an effete homosexual instead of an intrepid warrior. He wears skirts and lace, he is perfumed with cologne and surrounded by feathers, lanterns, and tiny mirrors in the solitude of his bedroom. This is located within a tower, and we immediately think of the Alhambra:

en el primer berberisco
de gritos y miradores.
[I:411]

Even the experimental "Oda al Santísimo Sacramento del Altar" shows some affinity with this miniature Lorcan world. As we have seen, the Host is presented as a "little tambourine of flour," enclosing a "diminutive and eternal Christ" (I:765-66). And though Lorca draws away from this atmosphere in *Poeta en Nueva York* and the *Llanto,* he returns to it in his last volume, *Diván del Tamarit.* Indeed, one of the Arab-Andalusian forms that inspired this book, the casida, was a kind of lyrical epigram. These poems, and Lorca's, "are the most paradoxical blend of extravagance with economy. . . . Casidas might be described as miniature Gongorisms."[17] Lorca's penchant for metaphor—the moment of insight that joins seemingly unrelated phenomena—might also be viewed as an aspect of his Arabic and Granadine inheritance. His metaphors, images, and symbols are like miniature star clusters within the constellations of individual poems.

The *Diván del Tamarit* is probably more openly Arabic and Granadine than any of the earlier works. Lorca's interpretation of Andalusian cities derives in part from an Islamic tradition in the Peninsula. As early as the thirteenth century, Granada, Cordova, and Seville were characterized by the poets of Al-Andalus in much the same manner as they appear in Lorca.[18] But as always, the poet excelled his sources. The Arabs eulogized cities as they praised beloved women.[19] Lorca's tone is normally not laudatory, but elegiac. His poetry expresses the deep layer of human emotion and tragedy beneath the surface of the major cities in Andalusia.

CORDOVA

Only two aspects of Lorca's Cordova will engage our attention here—its solitude and equilibrium—which also characterize this city in the verses of *cante jondo.* In the following poem, Cordova is associated with loneliness and a concomitant suffering:

> Entre Córdoba y Lucena
> hay una laguna clara
> donde lloraba mis penas
> cuando de ti me acordaba.[20]

Lorca exploits the city's reputation in his famous "Canción de jinete" and elsewhere, converting it into a kind of poetic myth. The two adjectives of the refrain,

> Córdoba.
> Lejana y sola,
> [I:313]

suggest the enormous measure of time and space that has lain upon the city for centuries. The horse and rider alone would be enough to hint at an impending tragedy in any Lorcan poem, but the presence of an ominous wind and the red moon of folk tradition seal the unlucky protagonist's fate. Indeed, horse, rider, and death form a recurrent group of images around Cordova in Lorca's poetry. Two notable examples are the hundred dead horsemen of the "Gráfico de la Petenera," buried among the olive groves, and the horse and rider of the "Romance del Emplazado," where the solitude, the patio with flowers, the lime, the cold wind, the dark mountains (perhaps the Sierra Morena?), and the equilibrium of the Emplazado's death indicate an unmistakably Cordovan atmosphere (I: 190, 195, 423-25). The "Romance de la pena negra," with its olives and somber mountains, may also belong to this sphere of Lorca's lyrical geography. Olives suggest Cordova and its province above all other places in Lorca's work; this region is even more typical of his poetic Andalusia than Granada. In the city of Seneca, Lucan, and Góngora, tragedy is neither a memory as in Granada, nor a presentiment as in Seville. It is alive and present. In contrast to Granada and Seville, Cordova does not reveal its spirit in dreams or laughter, but in noble monuments of architecture.

Beneath its Moorish surface, Lorca perceived the city's authentic Roman essence. This essence is both esthetic and ethical—a kind of stoicism, or "senequismo" in the language of the poet's Granadine predecessor, Ángel Ganivet.[21] It is curious to note in passing that in Cordova, *cante jondo* does not manifest itself through specific regional forms, but in a characteristic style or manner: a "solemn and sententious style, deliberate and static."[22] Lorca's Cordovan poetry seems to be another echo of this style. The protagonist of the "Romance del Emplazado," for example, dies according to the Senecan prescription: he accepts his strange fate and submits to its superior power without complaint. He dies with true Roman dignity:

> Y la sábana impecable,
> de duro acento romano,
> daba equilibrio a la muerte
> con las rectas de sus paños.

If this poem represents the moral character of Cordova, another ballad in the *Romancero gitano,* "San Rafael," represents its art. It corresponds to "San Miguel" (Granada) and "San Gabriel" (Seville) in the same volume. Raphael is the saint who personifies Cordova's fusion of diverse elements—Roman, Arabic, Spanish. A classic firmness counterbalances the city's evanescent fragility:

> pues si la sombra levanta
> la arquitectura del humo,
> un pie de mármol afirma
> su casto fulgor enjuto
> ....
> Blanda Córdoba de juncos.
> Córdoba de arquitectura.

Cordova contains a synthesis of past and present, heaven and earth, gods and men, the sublime and the banal:

> Y mientras el puente sopla
> diez rumores de Neptuno,
> vendedores de tabaco
> huyen por el roto muro.
> [I:412-13]

Lorca's verse here and in the whole *Romancero* also contains a synthesis: concrete and exact in form, mysterious and suggestive in content. More than any other city, Cordova symbolized for him the controlled passion he sought to express in his own art.

SEVILLE

Even Seville, the emblem of Andalusian wit, gracefulness, and *joie de vivre,* does not escape from the shadows cast by the birds of ill omen in Lorca's poetry. The *saeta* stands at one pole of Sevillian art, opposite the lighthearted *sevillanas.* Though this great city represents an island of joy in the middle of a tragic land, she is subject to invasion from the dark forces that lurk on the plain around her. Lorca suggests this in his beautiful little "Canto nocturno de los marineros andaluces" (I:778-79). Seville, along with Cadiz, Gibraltar, and Málaga, embodies lower, maritime Andalusia in the poem. What begins as an apparently innocent song gradually darkens as the typical Lorcan omens—lemons, knives, and the moon—gradually reveal themselves. The poem moves in a progression from the coast—Cadiz, Gibraltar, Málaga—to the interior—Seville, Carmona, the salt flats. The farther from the sea, the more foreboding the atmosphere becomes. Finally, the lyric speaker warns Cadiz and Seville, one bathed by the Atlantic and the other by the Guadalquivir, not to advance toward the dry and solitary hinterland—the land of anguish, with its intense, hopeless yearning for the sea.

Seville usually appears in Lorca's work, shimmering in light and color, as it does in the real world and in the verses of *cante jondo*. Her gypsy quarter of Triana has produced some great interpreters of *siguiriyas, soleares* and *saetas,* but the song that most typifies the city is the *sevillana*. Actually this form, a mere folk song used to accompany a dance of the same name, does not belong to the proper realm of *cante jondo*. However, Lorca himself wrote and harmonized one of these songs, and it is very indicative of his attitude toward the queen of Andalusian cities.

Sevillanas are normally performed during fairs and pilgrimages. A southern variety of the Castilian *seguidilla,* their infectious charm derives from the combination of a melody in duple rhythm with a dance and hand-clapping in triple time. Lorca's example offers a good idea of the form since it borrows almost entirely from popular versions.

1

¡Viva Sevilla!
Llevan las sevillanas
en la mantilla
un letrero que dice:
¡Viva Sevilla!

¡Viva Triana!
¡Vivan los trianeros,
los de Triana!
¡Vivan los sevillanos
y sevillanas!

2

Lo traigo andado.
La Macarena y todo
lo traigo andado.

Lo traigo andado;
cara como la tuya
no la he encontrado.

La Macarena y todo
lo traigo andado.

3

Ay río de Sevilla,
qué bien pareces
lleno de velas blancas
y ramas verdes.
[I:792-93]

Familiar by now are the Sevillian motifs of Holy Week (the Macarena), the Guadalquivir, color, and exaggeration. The sort of neighborhood pride contained in the first stanza is typical of the *sevillanas* and flamenco poetry in general. The second stanza in particular represents the traditional amorous poetry of Andalusia with its nearly blasphemous flattery. Compare it to this *sevillana* in which the speaker also praises his lady in a religious context:

La iglesia se ilumina
cuando tú entras,
y se llena de flores
cuando te sientas;

y cuando sales
se revisten de luto
"tós" los altares.[2]

Finally, the last stanza of Lorca's *sevillanas* contains a slight variation of a well-known *seguidilla* by Lope de Vega:

Río de Sevilla,
¡cuán bien pareces,
con galeras blancas
y ramos verdes!

All of the elegance, color, and movement of Seville seem to crystallize in these lines.

Since I have mentioned the ballads in the *Romancero gitano* that refer specifically to Granada and Cordova, I should not leave Seville without touching on her respective poem: "San Gabriel." The angel appears as a more manly version of Saint Michael, a beautiful young boy with slim waist and broad shoulders.

Un bello niño de junco,
anchos hombros, fino talle,
piel de nocturna manzana,
boca triste y ojos grandes,
nervio de plata caliente
ronda la desierta calle.
[I: 414-16]

The saint recalls the young gallant who makes rounds of the street where
his beloved lives, in this *sevillana:*

Un moreno garboso
ronda mi calle
y dice que me quiere
más que a su mare.[24]

In his patent leather shoes and embroidered vest, Gabriel is a fusion between a gypsy bullfighter and an Andalusian *señorito.* He addresses the
virgin as if she were a young beauty, in a parody of the Annunciation,
"Morena de maravilla." She is in turn a silly, sentimental adolescent. The
whole atmosphere of the poem gently ironizes the Sevillian character with
its frivolity, blasphemy, and grace, and its transformation of the divine into the human.

MÁLAGA AND JEREZ DE LA FRONTERA

In Lorca's poetry, Málaga never achieves the symbolic status of the three
main cities of Andalusia. Nevertheless, in at least one work, *Poema del
cante jondo,* it comes close to doing so. There is one poem in the volume
which deals specifically with Málaga, and another which celebrates one of
her greatest *cantaores.* "Malagueña" forms the first part of a series of
poems entitled "Tres ciudades"; the other two cities are Cordova and
Seville. It is important to note that this is the only fragment in the book,
with the exception of "Saeta," bearing the actual name of a genre of *cante
jondo.* Like the other poem, it approximates the traditional form in style
and content. *Malagueñas* are usually composed of four- or five-line stanzas with octosyllabic verses, but their interpretation is extremely free as
Lorca apparently understood. This is a traditional example of the song:

> Los peces se mueren de pena
> la mar se vistió de luto,
> los árboles no echan fruto
> porque ha muerto mi morena.[25]

As in this piece, the sea almost invariably appears. It gives the form its brilliance and movement, as well as its salty bitterness. The *malagueña* needs the sea in order to thrive, just as the *serrana* needs the mountains:

> ¿Ese cante malagueño,
> en dónde lo has "aprendío"?
> A la "oriyita" del mar,
> a la sombra de un navío.[26]

The bitterness of these songs may be related to the taste of death, pain, or disillusion in love:

> Eres tú como la adelfa,
> que da sombra en la ribera:
> con el corazón amargo,
> verde y colorá por fuera.[27]

The *malagueña* is emotional and elegiac. "Its common denominator is feeling. . . . Love, death, memory, nostalgia, and jealousy make up the affective world where the *malagueña* flourishes."[28] Like the *granadina,* it belongs to the *fandango* family. But in contrast to the song from Granada, it has outgrown its humble origin and become a more serious form. When interpreted well, it inclines toward a solemn, emotive style that puts it within the realm of *cante jondo* in the strictest sense.

Lorca was therefore justified in placing his "Malagueña" alongside of *siguiriyas* and *saetas* in the *Poema del cante jondo.*

> La muerte
> entra y sale
> de la taberna.
>
> Pasan caballos negros
> y gente siniestra
> por los hondos caminos
> de la guitarra.
>
> Y hay un olor a sal
> y a sangre de hembra,

en los nardos febriles
de la marina.

La muerte
entra y sale,
y sale y entra
la muerte
de la taberna.

[I:211]

The poem takes place in a tavern, or perhaps in a *café chantant*. The influence of the sea makes itself felt: salt smell and the "feverish spikenards" of the shore. This flower, characterized by its sterile and lethal fragrance, usually hints at an ominous presence in Lorca's poetry, often death or the moon.[29] The smell of "female blood" might vaguely remind us of the "Romance de la pena negra," with Soledad Montoya and her earthy odor of "horse and shadow." This poem with a Malagan setting has a sordid, visceral quality. Lorca seems to be interpreting the seamy side of flamenco life, the dark underworld of vice and crime that became associated with Andalusian music in the last part of the nineteenth century. (In our time, this turbid atmosphere has been replaced by a less tragic but equally vulgar commercial exploitation in the *tablaos* or flamenco clubs of major Spanish cities.) "Sinister people" and typically Lorcan horses move about this poem, as Death comes in and out the door of the tavern. The poet repeats the same simple idea in the opening and closing refrain, merely inverting the word order. The final, serpentining verses suggest the windings of the *malagueña*'s melody, and also the fatality of the act of Death: "the inevitability of Death's continually coming in and going out—over and over again—not in the concrete place of the tavern, but in the life of man and the work of the poet."[30]

Another short lyric in the *Poema del cante jondo* carries the name of Juan Breva, the legendary Malagan *cantaor,* in its title. Born in the middle of the last century, he became famous above all for his original interpretation of the *malagueña*, "sad and lovely as an elegy."[31]

Juan Breva tenía
cuerpo de gigante
y voz de niña.
Nada como su trino.
Era la misma
pena cantando

detrás de una sonrisa.
Evoca los limonares
de Málaga la dormida,
y hay en su llanto dejos
de sal marina.
Como Homero cantó
ciego. Su voz tenía,
algo de mar sin luz
y naranja exprimida.
[I:204]

The leitmotif of this poem is the bitterness previously mentioned: sea salt, *pena,* lemon groves, a squeezed orange. These fruits evoke the warmth of Málaga's sun and the indolence of an ancient Mediterranean port, but their colorful rind encloses an acid juice. A polarity between opposites forms the structural skeleton of the poem: Juan Breva's huge body and his fragile voice; his smiling countenance and the pain in his song; the sweetness and the bitterness of Málaga's fruits and by extension, of life there. These opposites also reveal the spirit of the *malagueña,* an Andalusian example of Shelley's verse, "Our sweetest songs are those that tell of saddest thoughts."

Other cities of Andalusia, even some that are important parts of the flamenco world—like Cadiz and Huelva—shine by their absence in Lorca's poetry. They were probably too shallow and raucous for his taste, too flooded by the fickle optimism of the sea. (Málaga is also a coastal city, but when the wind from the interior blows—significantly called the *terral*—a leaden seriousness is said to possess her inhabitants.) For similar reasons perhaps, the lucidity of the Spanish Levant failed to attract Lorca. Moreover, this region lies beyond the natural area where *cante jondo* is performed. Only one of the eighteen ballads in the *Romancero gitano* may take place in a Levantine atmosphere, and even this is not definite: "La monja gitana," with its blinding sunlight, luxuriant vegetation and spices, and its sensual, Mediterranean silences (I:404-05).

One final Andalusian city claims our attention: Jerez de la Frontera, the nominal scene of the great "Romance de la Guardia Civil española." Jerez is located in the very heart of the flamenco country and has nourished some monumental figures in the history of *cante jondo.* Above them all towers the legendary, Pharaonic Manuel Torres, "Niño de Jerez." Lorca was an admirer of this gypsy singer, and to him he dedicated his series of "Viñetas flamencas" in the *Poema del cante jondo*

(I: 201-08). The poet had good reason to place his "city of the gypsies" in Jerez, since its quarters of Santiago and Puerta del Sol are heavily populated by that race.

The action of the poem occurs during a spring fiesta. The city rises above the plain like a vision from a fairy tale: towers of cinnamon and smell of musk, lanterns and green lights, flags and banners, half-moon and pumpkin. The semi-Oriental atmosphere may be related to the Asiatic origin of the gypsies, to the echoes of the Old Testament in the poem, or to its mythic nature. Even in the midst of the city's rejoicing, Lorca laments for Jerez as if she had been destroyed in a remote past:

> ¡Oh ciudad de los gitanos!
> ¿Quién te vio y no te recuerda?
> Ciudad de dolor y almizcle,
> con las torres de canela.

The invasion by the Guardia Civil parallels the sacking of Bethlehem by Roman centurions—

> En el Portal de Belén
> los gitanos se congregan

or a Sabine rape—

> Rosa la de los Camborios,
> gime sentada en su puerta
> con sus dos pechos cortados
> puestos en una bandeja.
> Y otras muchachas corrían
> perseguidas por sus trenzas
> . . . . [32]

In this, the last of the specifically gypsy ballads in the *Romancero,* the Andalusia of maps and atlases dissipates in an ideal realm of legend and poetry. In the final verses, the poet repeats his original invocation and says,

> ¡Oh ciudad de los gitanos!
> ¿Quién te vio y no te recuerda?
> Que te busquen en mi frente.
> Juego de luna y arena.
> [I:426-30]

To find the poetic land inhabited by Lorca's gypsies, we must search for it in this "play of moon and sand," heaven and earth, vision and reality.

The poet's mythic Andalusia belongs to an artistic tradition in Spain. Hispano-Arabic poetry offered him a possible model for his lyrics on Granada, Cordova, and Seville. Lorca's Andalusia belongs to the Arabic legacy, though he went far beyond this and his other sources. After the Hispano-Arabic period, the theme of Andalusia did not reappear in Peninsular letters until very late. This was probably due to the peculiar nature of regional feeling there. In contrast to other major areas of Spain, Andalusia never constituted an autonomous political unit after the Arab presence. This land certainly does not lack an individual character; Spaniards and foreigners have normally considered it the most exotic and un-European part of the country. But in spite of its uniqueness and its past of ancient cultures, historically Andalusia is an extension of Castile. It was incorporated directly into the Spanish nation as a result of the reconquest. Now literary regionalism in the Peninsula began with the Romantics' interest in medieval Spain and was essentially a defense of each area's specific qualities against the unifying tendencies of the modern world. Thus the regional writers of the nineteenth century were traditionalists almost by definition. Andalusia, with its sparse history of medieval Christianity, had little to offer them. Zorrilla, imitating Hugo's *Orientales,* chose to evoke the Arabic past of his country. Bécquer was the first in a long line of poets, leading to Juan Ramón Jiménez and Lorca, who would reject the kind of picturesque and exotic Andalusia portrayed by Zorrilla.[33]

The discovery of the literary possibilities of this and other regions of Spain belongs in part to the *costumbrista* writers as well as to the Romantics. Like most movements in Spanish letters, *costumbrismo* probably began under a foreign impetus, recognizing models such as Jouy in France, Addison and Steele in England. Moreover, the journals of travelers in the Peninsula, such as that of Théophile Gautier, brought Spaniards' attention to the national beauties which they had failed to exploit themselves. Estébanez Calderón's *Escenas andaluzas* (1847) was one of the first, and remained the best of the *costumbrista* works that dealt with Andalusia. The author even described some songs and interpreters of *cante jondo* in a few of his lively sketches, as well as other manifestations of local life. The creators of the Andalusian regional novel—Fernán Caballero, Alarcón, and Valera—would undergo the influence of the

Escenas andaluzas. But we obviously should not seek Lorca's sources in these writers. The *costumbristas* had the virtue of rediscovering the reality of Spanish life, as José F. Montesinos has clearly shown;[34] yet they usually saw that reality through a distorting glass of formal morality, the picturesque or quaint. Without losing sight of the great differences between them, we should note the parallel between the *costumbristas'* attempt to preserve the traditional monuments and customs of Spain, and the efforts of Falla and Lorca to save the ancient Andalusian song.

Lorca's Andalusia belongs in part to a modern lyrical trajectory that began with Salvador Rueda, the Malagan poet often associated with the beginnings of Modernism in Spain. From Rueda to Juan Ramón Jiménez, passing through Manuel Machado, this trajectory describes an arc from the local to the universal, though remaining essentially Andalusian. It must be admitted that in one respect, Lorca's poetry seems to return to the merely local manifestations of his native region which Juan Ramón had eliminated almost entirely from his verse. If the latter poet evolved what has been called an "andalucismo universal," Lorca created an "andalucismo profundo."[35] Neither the Arabic quality of his imagination nor the regional motifs, not even the popular air of his style can adequately define Lorca's deep Andalusian essence. In contrast to the Romantics, the *costumbristas*, and the Modernists, this essence is profound rather than superficial. It resides in his fundamental attitude to life and art, in an almost pagan cult of the earth, an acute sense of human tragedy—united to a refined, graceful feeling for expression.

Chapter Six

The Mythic Man: The Gypsy

Just as Andalusia provides the typical setting, the gypsy is the archetypal inhabitant of Lorca's poetic land. This fact would be of little importance to us if the gypsies did not also play an essential role in the world of *cante jondo*. They have made up a large proportion of the best interpreters of this music since the eighteenth century. The attitude toward life known as "flamenco" manifests itself above all in the members of this race. More than a style of music or dance, this attitude represents an "integral way of feeling the cosmos and the small world of one's own personality."[1] To a certain degree, the characters of the *Romancero gitano* incarnate such a vital posture, but the importance of the gypsies in Lorca's work goes far beyond the scope of *cante jondo*. The poet believed this people to be the most representative of his native region: "We Andalusians all have something of the gypsy in us," he said (II: 887). Lorca's gypsies might stand for dispossessed and marginal human groups anywhere in the world.

As we have seen, the poet's lyrical Andalusia constitutes a fertile ground for the flowering of myth. In the same way, the gypsies portrayed in his *Romancero* tend to embody a mythic vision of the world. Their basic instincts, atavistic fears, and violent actions transport us to a remote past in which reason has still not replaced emotion and intuition. The tragedy of life unfolds in a conflict between human and nonhuman powers; man achieves dignity in a struggle for self-assertion against unequal forces. This conflict evokes a legendary past, but also has a real impact on the present. Lorca attempted to "harmonize *gypsy mythology* with the purely ordinary life of the present day. . . ."[2] The protagonists of the *Romancero* struggle against the hostile powers of fate; they also defend themselves against an oppressive law, morality, and social order. In this sense, Lorca's book dramatizes the conflict between the mythic imagination and modern ideas.[3]

Gustavo Correa has seen the characteristic quality of the *Romancero gitano* in its alternation and fusion of two planes of reality, one human and existential, the other legendary and mythic.[4] A concrete anecdote usually gives the ballads their dynamic impulse: the death of a child, woman, or man, a blood feud, a seduction, a raid by the Guardia Civil. Through the incantation of the word, the transpositions of metaphor, and a ritual stylization of action, this everyday reality becomes part of a higher realm. At the same time, nature and superhuman elements participate in the realization of human destiny.

In "La casada infiel," an apparently vulgar amorous conquest is transformed into an event of mythic proportions. Everything is metamorphosed in the pregnant atmosphere of this poem:

> Sin luz de plata en sus copas
> los árboles han crecido.

The trees grow, and the married woman's body, through figurative language, mingles with the natural, animal, and celestial worlds (spikenards, conch shell, glass, moon, fishes, fire, filly):

> Ni nardos ni caracolas
> tienen el cutis tan fino,
> ni los cristales con luna
> relumbran con tanto brillo.
> Sus muslos se me escapaban
> como peces sorprendidos,
> la mitad llenos de lumbre,
> la mitad llenos de frío.
> Aquella noche corrí
> el mejor de los caminos,
> montado en potra de nácar
> sin bridas y sin estribos.
> [I: 406-07]

In the "Muerte de Antoñito el Camborio," the gypsy protagonist acquires a mythic profile in his almost superhuman defense of his life. He takes on the attributes of a wild boar, a dolphin, a horse, a flower, and again, the moon:

> Les clavó sobre las botas
> mordiscos de jabalí.
> En la lucha daba saltos
> jabonados de delfín
> . . . .

Antonio Torres Heredia,
Camborio de dura crin,
moreno de verde luna,
voz de clavel varonil

. . . .

Just as men rise to the height of gods, superhuman figures descend to participate in the hero's death:

Un ángel marchoso pone
su cabeza en un cojín.
Otros de rubor cansado
encendieron un candil.
[I: 419-20]

In the last chapter we saw the interaction between the protagonists of Lorca's poetry and their lyrical background. Here we witness a mutual attraction between the same protagonists and superhuman figures, another essential aspect of the mythic universe.

The heroes of Lorca's *Romancero* often resemble men-gods, whose bravery and sacrificial deaths appease the fates and ensure the survival of the people. As Luis Rosales has pointed out, the ballads contain repeated allusions to the supernatural origin of the gypsies. They "accept their destiny as pagan gods and with it their irreparable tragic end."[5] Moreover, the recurrent conflicts between this people and the Guardia Civil echo the struggle between gods and men in ancient mythology. The adventures of the gypsies parallel the legendary thefts and abductions of golden oranges, cows, and virgins.[6]

Some of the themes we have noticed in *cante jondo* and in Lorca's poetry are of specifically gypsy origin: for example, *pena negra* and the fascination with blood. The title and form of the *Llanto por Ignacio Sánchez Mejías* may have been inspired by the gypsy funeral lament. The poem has some of the ritual, incantatory quality of primitive song, and has even been recited in the style of the *siguiriya gitana*.[7] The gypsies' laments are invested with great secrecy and performed spontaneously. When we hear this description of their traditional laments, we can hardly avoid recalling Lorca's *Llanto:* "intoned chants in a bass voice which sing to the repose of the dead person and vaunt his virtues."[8]

Some of the subjects discussed later could also be related to the gypsies, such as the *saeta*. Here I will develop just two of the more important echoes of this people's life as reflected in Lorca's poetry and *cante jondo*.

ANIMISM AND RELIGION

The gypsies of our world and Lorca's *Romancero gitano* possess a basically animistic attitude toward nature. Plants and animals, the elements, and the heavenly bodies have life and powers of their own. Though he may no longer be a vagabond, the gypsy remains sensitive to the messages of the earth and the seasons that are indispensable to nomadic races. Even his everyday language contains images and metaphors reflecting vivid mental states. For Lorca, this people incarnated the kind of imagination that created the primitive Andalusian song, *cante jondo.*

The gypsy's morbid fear of the wind offers an example of his animistic feelings. At one time, his fear was arguably motivated by the havoc this element must have wrought on his people's caravans. The wind has a clearly negative sign in the *Poema del cante jondo.* It crosses the air of the book with an ominous ripple, turning the weather vanes of towers and steeples, driving dust over the parched land. In the *Romancero*, the wind is personified in "Preciosa y el aire" (I: 395-97). It represents a sexual aggressor, as in some verses of flamenco poetry. This is a traditional example cited by Lorca in his first lecture:

> Tengo celos del aire
> que da en tu cara,
> si el aire fuera hombre
> yo lo matara.
> [I: 988]

In his own ballad, the wind takes on a form derived from gypsy mythology: a lecherous giant who wields a sword of obvious erotic connotations.[9] Perhaps he embodies a mere fantasy of the young gypsy girl who literally tempts her seducer by playing a tambourine alone on the mountain in the dead of night. Lorca was fully conscious of the gypsies' mythic attitude toward the wind, as we know from his lecture. His poem recalls the legendary atmosphere of an episode from Ovid's *Metamorphoses,* the wind replacing Apollo as the pursuer of the girl. She is not transformed into a laurel as in the Roman poem, though this tree does appear in the ballad. Lorca's version of the ancient myth ends in a burlesque anticlimax: the English consul gives Preciosa a glass of warm milk to calm her nerves.

Another case of animism has to do with water. The gypsies feel the same kind of phobia for this element as for the wind, although their camps are traditionally pitched on dry land. They have such a strong aversion to the sea that they rarely inhabit ports. Few gypsies are fishermen, none sailors. Jean-Paul Clébert tells the story of a Romanichal who once said to him, "If I give myself a wash, I no longer feel the man."[10] In this respect, we might think of Soledad Montoya in the "Romance de la pena negra," with her odor of "horse and shadow" and her desire to forget the sea. Indeed, the *Romancero gitano*, as well as the *Poema del cante jondo*, the *Llanto*, and *Diván del Tamarit*, portray an essentially landlocked world. From the time of his youthful writings, Lorca expressed an apprehension about water, especially that of cisterns and wells. In his early prose he evokes the "fearful cisterns in which the water has the tragic mystery of an intimate drama," and a "great cistern, fearful and deep" (I: 882, 885). Both of these passages refer to Granada. Perhaps Lorca's Granadine experience could partly explain his fascination with closed bodies of water; the city is full of wells, fountains, and pools. He undoubtedly drew from flamenco poetry also, in which water and suffering are often connected to each other, as in this *soleá:*

> ¡Qué grande es la pena mía,
> que me he caío en un poso
> y no encuentro la salía![11]

In European folklore, stagnant water can be the dwelling place of malefic spirits.[12] Lorca's insight happens to coincide with popular beliefs and soon surpasses them. His attitude toward water would be as difficult to define as the section entitled "Death by Water" in T. S. Eliot's *Waste Land.* Like Eliot's, Lorca's treatment of water is ambiguous and complex. He expressed a yearning for the openness and freedom of the sea, yet he possessed a strange fear of closed bodies of water. In them he seems to have sensed the inescapable circle of fate, the ultimate guilty chambers of the unconscious, and the irresistible call of death.[13]

To a certain extent, Lorca's poetry expresses the substrate of fears and emotions that underlies the gypsies' animistic beliefs. Thus the mythic ambiance of the *Poema del cante jondo* represents a primitive world in which hostile forces strive for ascendance. In the *Romancero gitano*, three poems dedicated to the patron saints of Granada, Cordova, and Seville tenderly burlesque the gypsies' gaudy taste for religious decoration and their occasional hysterical worship. The voice in these ballads does not belong to the poet, of course, but to an imaginary gypsy speaker whose mentality is reflected in the flamboyant style. In the "Romance de San Gabriel," for example, we saw how Lorca depicts the Visitation as it might be seen through the semipagan eyes of a Romanichal. He continues the parody in the "Romance de la Guardia Civil española," inventing a kind of flamenco Virgin and Saint Joseph (I: 426-30). In these two ballads, the mixture of respect and familiarity, devotion and blasphemy is typical of the gypsies' religious practice, and to a lesser extent, of Andalusians and Spaniards in general. The concrete, plastic expression of faith we saw in the *saeta* may also have undergone the influence of this people. The gypsies have always shown a propensity for lavish adornment, plasticity, and color in their religious rites. Lorca's poetry displays a preference for a concrete expression of religion, true to the spirit of the people he considered to be the most representative inhabitants of his native land.

INNATE SURREALISM

Though my purpose is to explore the influence of the traditional Andalusian song on Lorca's verse, we should not lose sight of the fact that he was also a poet of the twentieth century. Few members of his generation absorbed the innovations of vanguardist literature more completely. I do not intend to broach the subject of his literary sources. Only one of the many movements which left a trace on his poetry concerns us here, because of its possible connection with the gypsies—surrealism. His debt to the surrealist movement, founded by André Breton, has been adequately established by critics.[14] In the gypsies' art and view of life, Lorca may have glimpsed a sort of innate surrealism which fully harmonized with the poetic discoveries of the 1920s.

Perhaps the fact that Lorca began to employ his new lyrical techniques in the *Romancero gitano* was not merely accidental. A return to the stylization of primitive art constituted one of the basic elements of surrealism, along with a generally rebellious attitude, a free use of metaphor, and an attempt to express the activity of the unconscious through random images. As we know, Lorca found a poetical archetype of primitive man in the Andalusian gypsy. Rafael Lafuente has affirmed that the psychology of this race contains a kind of incipient surrealism.[15] Many of their poems display a boldness of language and imagination worthy of Lorca himself. The almost cinematic lucidity of some gypsy poetry must have attracted his attention:

> Con las fatiguitas de la muerte
> a un laíto yo me arrimé.
> Con los deítos de la mano
> arañaba la pared.[16]

These lines suggest the harsh, nightmarish light of many scenes in the *Romancero gitano*:

> Una dura luz de naipe
> recorta en el agrio verde,
> caballos enfurecidos
> y perfiles de jinetes.
> [I:398]

The gypsies' songs reflect vivid mental states beyond the limits of reason:

> Toítas las arañas negras
> qu'están metía'n sus níos,
> me pique'n er corasón,
> si mi queré es fingío.[17]

In Lorca's volume, the constant oscillation between the local and the cosmic, matter and spirit, the real and the imaginary, responds to a similar mental process. We move from actual Spanish cities—Málaga, Jerez de la Frontera—to a magic realm of balconies and towers of cinnamon; from real men of flesh and blood—Pedro Domecq, the English consul—to disembodied phantoms like the Amargo and Don Pedro; from the colorful saints of Andalusian folklore to the unworldly angels who administer to dead heroes.[18]

In addition to their poetry, the gypsies' style of life might also be called surrealist. Here the term does not refer to a literary school. Nothing could be farther from the truth. Behind the formal innovations of Breton and his followers, there was an aspiration toward a specific mode of behavior. In a lecture delivered at the Residencia de Estudiantes of Madrid in 1925, possibly attended by Lorca, Louis Aragon declared: "We place a curse on science, the twin sister of work. . . . I will never work. My hands preserve their purity."[19] These emphatic words are not far from the paradisiac ideal of many gypsies and some Spaniards—their defiance, their scorn for machines and the tyranny of labor, their "vegetative" existence. Being a Romanichal—or a "flamenco"—means foregoing certain comforts in exchange for the freedom to explore one's own person and feelings:

Vengo a buscar lo que busco,
mi alegría y mi persona.
[I:408]

Condemned to lead a miserable life in a world that does not conform to his own Edenic instincts, the gypsy dedicates his energy to what alone is fundamental and serious: his self and his own authentic existence. "The gypsy's whole obsession is to be himself or, as Lorca puts it, to behave 'like a legitimate gypsy,' in accordance with the basic spontaneity of his nature, the assertion of which gives substance and meaning to his life."[20]

Thus the practical dimensions of the surrealist program consisted of a desire to receive life as a natural gift without having to earn it by work. The philosophic intention of the movement was to discover the deeper realities behind sensory impressions; the senses cannot penetrate the profound causes of life. Breton and Aragon chose criminals and outcasts as their heroes, in this way affirming human innocence. Lorca preferred the gypsies, who stand for all marginal races and for man as a whole. They call themselves *Rom*, meaning the men, the archetype of the species. The surrealists defended the demands of the spirit, rebelling simultaneously against reason and society. The poet's helpless gypsies try to protect themselves against the Guardia Civil and the rational, inhuman order it represents. The surrealist experience culminates in the exaltation of darkness and the nocturnal regions of the psyche. We seem to have reached the lunar realm of *cante jondo* and the *Romancero gitano*.

Lorca was not a gypsy, of course, but a highly refined and cultured poet. If he treated this people in a few of his books, his intuition surpassed what they could offer him in flesh and blood. Besides, the subject matter of poetry is only a starting point, never sufficient grounds for judging its merit. Lorca transformed a small human group into a universal symbol which soars above the reality in which it was inspired. The gypsies of our world, for all the ancient sadness we divine in their visages, will never be as innocent or passionate as their lyrical brothers in the *Romancero gitano*.

Chapter Seven

Myth and History: The *Saeta*

As we have seen, the *saeta* probably left a greater impression on Lorca's poetry than any other form of *cante jondo*. In order to reveal the mythic roots of traditional Andalusian music, I will discuss at some length the history of the *saeta*. Then we will be prepared to see how Lorca interprets this religious song in his *Poema del cante jondo*.

Each spring, as Lorca says, the *saeta* leaves "tracks of warm lilies" in the skies of Andalusian towns and cities. During the early morning hours of Maundy Thursday and Good Friday, the people offer these songs of contrition and love to the Christs and Virgins in the traditional processions of Holy Week. Notwithstanding its beauty and its continued vitality, the *saeta* is one of the least known genres of popular Spanish poetry. Extravagant conjectures have been made about its music, at the general expense of its poetry—a much surer point of departure.

The *saeta* is a kind of musical prayer, sung without accompaniment to the wooden images in Spanish Easter processions. The Andalusian is the most well known variety, as well as the richest in musical and poetic value. Though many kinds of traditional religious poetry have been included in the genre, only one—the *saeta* of Christ's Passion—is sung during Holy Week in public places. In contrast to the *copla* and *villancico*, the *saeta* usually consists of a single stanza without refrain; unlike these two songs, it is never choral, and is only performed during Easter. As the floats or *pasos* slowly rock down streets and alleys on litters borne by penitents, surrounded by the hooded members of a particular lay brotherhood, a man or woman lifts his voice in plaintive song from a window or balcony. The procession halts until the melody has ended, then trumpets sound and the solemn march continues. As the sculptured images of the crucified Christ or the Mater Dolorosa move away over the heads of the crowd, the emotion of that instant remains in the dawn air; like all expressions of *duende*, it will never be exactly repeated.

Musically, the *saeta* has the ritual quality of ancient song due to its use of semitones and a fluctuation between the major and minor modes.[1] As Lorca noted in his first lecture, these are characteristics of Andalusian music in general. Though the *saeta* represents a uniquely religious form of *cante jondo*, it is clearly related to genres such as the *toná* and *siguiriya*.[2]

The poetry of the *saeta* shows a dramatic intimacy and a painful identification with Christ's suffering:

> ¿Quién me presta una escalera
> para subir al madero,
> para quitarle los clavos
> a Jesús el Nazareno?[3]

As here, the commonest metric form is the eight-syllable quatrain with assonance in the even lines. The *saeta* of five verses is also frequent, less so that of six or more lines. The rhyme scheme varies greatly. In general the *saeta* is a very free form with much improvisation. It is literally impossible to hear an identical interpretation of a given poem, even by the same singer.

The theme of Mary's sorrow is as prevalent as that of the Passion. Many of the numerous Andalusian Virgins are invoked: the Macarena, the Virgen de las Angustias, Our Lady of Sorrows, Our Lady of Solitude. Besides episodes from the Gospel—the Last Supper, the seizing of Jesus, Calvary—several apocryphal legends are treated, such as the Veronica, or the swallows who remove the thorns from Christ's forehead:

> Ya bienen las golondrinas
> con su pico muy sereno
> pa' quitarle las espinas
> a Jesús er Nazareno.[4]

The *saeta*'s lingering over the physical details of the Crucifixion has become almost proverbial. It is related in part to the style of the splendid Baroque figures of polychromatic wood carried by the brotherhoods in the processions. But the morbidity of the *saeta* often exceeds these images, whose movement it may describe:

> Míralo, por donde viene
> el mejor de los nacidos
> . . . .[5]

> Mira ese cadáver frío,
> desos tres clavos pendiente,
> todo llagado y herido:
> en su costado una fuente
> que el pecado ha redimido.[6]

The *saeta* addresses God with an intimacy that would astonish north European and Protestant ears. It does not penetrate the precinct of the divine on a winding Jacob's ladder, nor by the arduous threefold path of the mystics, but directly, in a straight line, on the wings of its melody. Hence its name: *saeta*, an arrow. It carries the "collective pulse of the multitude, thronged into the street, the plaza, the church, transfixed with a spontaneous fervor and wounded by an ineffable religious feeling."[7] The singer and listeners undergo an emotional catharsis in contact with the divine sacrifice, Christ's suffering fusing with man's. For the people present, everlasting life is actually being achieved in the death of that God-man.[8] Unfortunately, the modern *saeta* has degenerated to a degree, especially in the major cities. From a natural religious expression of the people, it has gradually become a weapon of the political, social, and ecclesiastic hierarchy whose purpose is to maintain the appearances of a devout and picturesque Spain. Lorca did not live to see this new development. Even in the modern *saeta*, the old emotion still palpitates beneath the verses.

The greatest defect of these songs is a sentimentality that often approaches the lachrymose. The singer of *saetas* chooses to depict the same aspect of God—grotesque and bloody—as many popular sculptors and painters in the Hispanic world, an antithesis of the sublime, peaceful Christ of Velázquez.

Like the birth of lyric poetry in Spain, the problem of the *saeta*'s origin has received three basic interpretations: Arabic, Jewish, and Christian. The supporters of the Arabic hypothesis believe there may be a connection between the *saeta* and the muezzin's cries of prayer hours, for example. Only one scholar, Arcadio de Larrea, has described in some detail this possible relation with Arabic music, specifically with the popular songs of Morocco. In Lorca's first lecture he noted that some folk melodies from northern Africa are still known as "songs of the Moors from Granada." Larrea says of a *siguiriya* and a *saeta* analyzed by him: "It is not possible to deny their close similarity with the typical songs of Moroccan folklore. The primitive tonal modes attest to this similarity as well as the enharmonic intervals . . . the simple rhythm, the narrow acoustic range in which the melody unfolds, and the varied vocal inflections."[9] But the author himself rejects the Arabic hypothesis, leaning on the authority of the Sevillian composer Joaquín Turina. Until more concrete musical examples are brought forth, the idea of Arabic influence can only illumine some general tendencies of the *saeta*, which are pervasive in Spanish poetry as a whole: an intimacy with the divine, a kind of sensuous realism or stress on physical details—themes explored by Américo Castro.

The Hebrew hypothesis is slightly more fertile. According to it, the *saeta* derives from a fourteenth- or fifteenth-century Sephardic rendition of the *Kol Nidrei* prayer.[10] In it the newly converted Jew begs Jehovah to annul his abjuration of the Mosaic law and his profession of Christian faith made under pressure from the Inquisition. This prayer is believed to have been a means of communication among those *conversos* who continued to practice the old religion in secret. According to this theory, the fusion of a feeling of unworthiness and contrition with a descriptive sensuousness would have passed on to the *saeta*.

As in the arguments that sustain the Arabic hypothesis, historical facts are lacking here. Moreover, to "pretend, without very certain proofs of the fact, that a song performed in the middle of a congregation of the faithful was a secret means of communication, precisely during the commemoration of Jesus' death at the hands of the Jews, by persons who were obviously suspicious and in front of an adversary of the greatest mental acuteness, such as the Andalusian, is equivalent to reaching for the moon."[11] In fact, the Hebrews' responsibility for the Crucifixion is one of the most common motifs in the *saeta:*

> En la caye 'e l'Amargura
> se cayó Su Majestá,
> y aqueyos perros judíos
> lo alebantan a patás.[12]

Nevertheless, we should remember that some of the fiercest diatribes against the Jews in the fifteenth and sixteenth centuries were written by *conversos*. A single fact can be a double-edged sword, serving to demonstrate or refute the notion of Hebrew influence. There existed such diversity of belief and conduct among Spanish Jews that it is dangerous to attribute uniform tendencies to them. "From this group of mystics and apostates, of passionate poets and cold men of law, it is not easy to extract a common denominator, temperamental or ideological."[13] Yet the weight of their contribution to Spanish culture in this period forces us to broach the subject.

In favor of the Jewish hypothesis is the similar relation between the *hassan* who intones the prayers in synagogues and the congregation who hears him, and the *saetero* and his public. Both singers hold the prestige of mediators between God and the faithful. Their art is accordingly intricate and difficult to master, and they embody the collective spirit of the multitude. The importance of the *conversos* in Spanish poetry during a crucial period for the development of the *saeta* (as I will show later)—1450 to 1550—is another point in favor of this hypothesis. Lyric poetry may have offered an escape for the expression of feelings of loss and anguish engendered in some of them by their new condition. Indeed, certain *saetas* seem to be motivated more by the singer's suffering than by pity for Jesus or Mary. The *carcelera*, for example, is a special variety sung by prisoners:

> Virgen de la Soledad
> no te pases tan serena;
> echa tu vista a la cárcel,
> quita grillos y cadenas.[14]

What one notices here is the affliction in the singer's voice, the representation of life as something difficult, a literal or figurative jail. The famous verse cited earlier—"¿Quién me presta una escalera . . . ?"—now suggests a double meaning to us: flight from a world of sorrow and union with God in the beyond.

Although it offers several possible approaches, the Hebrew theory clashes with a serious obstacle. The genesis of the *saeta* was probably medieval, but the first known reference to it dates from the late seventeenth century and its maturation occurred in the eighteenth and nineteenth. By 1700 the descendants of *conversos* had little consciousness as a class and had been largely absorbed in the mass of Spanish society. The Jews could not have played a major part in the development of this song, though they may have contributed to its creation.

The Christian hypothesis holds that the *saeta* grew out of the liturgy of the Church and the religious drama of the Middle Ages. There were already glimmerings of this idea in the last century. One of the first collectors of Spanish folk songs, Emilio Lafuente y Alcántara, saw a relation between the *saeta* and Easter Passion plays.[15] Adolfo Salazar believed the song descended from the ejaculatory prayers of early Catholic liturgy; these were short, fervent utterances "directed toward heaven as if propelled by the heartfelt impulse of the penitent."[16] Once they had spread across Spain as Easter songs or *calvarios*, they would have acquired a peculiar character in Andalusia under the influence of *cante jondo*. Neither Salazar nor anyone else has been able to describe this final process, called *flamenquización*. Documents are lacking to trace this hypothetical but potentially crucial stage in the growth of the *saeta*.

In our own time we have seen how the responses of a congregation can create a musical atmosphere charged with ecstatic zeal: in the black Protestant churches of the southern United States. That *saetas* have a certain dramatic and liturgical nature is beyond doubt. Some even refer to the interior of churches:

> Un árbol en la iglesia
> con espinas y sin flor;
> en cada ramito un ángel
> y en medio nuestro Señor.

Others, as we have seen, depict postures, gestures, and characters in action:

> Por ayí biene San Juan
> con er dedo señalando,
> en busca de su Maestro,
> que lo ban crucificando.[17]

Still others, fortunately not as numerous, are frankly moralizing and reverberate with echoes of the pulpit:

> Contempla aquí a tu Señor
> desnudo y avergonzado
> y duramente azotado,
> sólo por tenerte amor.[18]

This example is clearly more literary than the others and is one of the few cases of consonant rhyme. If the liturgical theory contains some truth, the tone of the *saetas* would have become less formal and more popular as they spread outside the walls of the church. How and when this might have happened will be seen later.

The last and most ingenious theory on the origin of the *saeta* is Arcadio de Larrea's "ritual hypothesis." According to this musicologist, the *saeta* is the "survival of a remote fertility rite that was performed by a violent sacrifice, Christianized in its present form and stripped of its primitive ideology, whose most recent explanation we find in Vedic tradition."[19] Like the primitive rites of spring, the *saeta* does indeed have a cyclic quality. Holy Week celebrations in Spain are not mere reflections of a two-thousand-year-old event: they reenact a drama that is always new, with a real significance for the present. The Andalusians say that Christ *dies* on Good Friday, and *is resurrected* on Easter Sunday. The verses of the *saeta* transpire this feeling of actuality: "Míralo, por allí viene." Larrea says that the music itself contains a symbolic system of tones that represents a life-death symbolism. The Indian Upanishads would be the prototype of this symbolism. Vedic tradition divides its sacred chant into five parts which are repeated in the five phrases of many *saetas*. As in the latter, the singer adopts an ecstatic posture and releases his shrill voice in a violent outburst, clenching his fists. The song itself is like an arrow that pierces the air as it celebrates the supreme sacrifice.

Larrea recognizes the danger of explaining the phenomena of one culture by those of another, but there seem to be some confirmations of his hypothesis in the verses of many *saetas*. The motif of blood, for example, goes far beyond a realistic description or doctrine of redemption. Christ's face, hair, eyes, hands, and feet are literally bathed in blood in numerous *saetas*. It falls to the earth, stains a rock or the face of the grief-stricken Virgin, or is caught in silver chalices by the three Marys:

> Ya vienen las tres Marías
> con cálices de plata
> para recoger la sangre
> que Jesucristo derrama.[20]

Could this be related to the pagan taboo on the spilling of royal blood, in this case the King of Kings? It is a common rule in primitive societies that royal blood not be spilled on the earth. The explanation probably lies in the belief that the soul resides in the body fluid.[21] Christ's blood is not only capable of redeeming the sinner, but of fecundating nature, and his sacrifice ensures the renewal of spring:

> Jazmines de luna nueva
> le nacieron a la Cruz,
> y claveles, a la tierra

que echaron las manos buenas
en la tumba de Jesús.[22]

The cross is a tree, the divine wounds and Christ become flowers:

Mira una rosa é pasión:
cuéntale siete puñales,
una corona d'espinas
y tres clabitos mortales.[23]

Perhaps Larrea is correct in referring the origin of the *saeta* to an ancient seasonal rite, but he may have gone too far afield in searching for its roots. Although the Vedic tradition could have been carried from India to Spain by the gypsies, a closer antecedent might be found in the Mediterranean cults that were directly replaced by Christianity. The first Christian communities developed in the midst of Oriental peoples such as the Semites, Phrygians, and Egyptians. The pagan elements preserved by the new faith derived from the cults of these peoples with which it coexisted for hundreds of years. Saint Augustine, in the fifth century, still knew the ancient fertility rites at first hand. Perhaps Larrea could not find any musical examples to support his theory from the peoples who worshipped the Syrian god Tammuz, the Egyptian Osiris, the Phrygian Attis, or the Greek Adonis. The cult of Attis for example included numerous elements that seem to foreshadow Spanish Easter celebrations: the time of year (March 22-24) and the three-day cycle; the bearing of the sacrificed god on a tree-cross by members of a guild; the sounding of trumpets; and the symbolism of flowers and blood.[24] The worship of Attis had already won wide acceptance in Rome by the first century A.D. This and the other Mediterranean cults traveled to the farthest bounds of the Roman Empire with the foreign legionaries, and later became disguised beneath a Christian exterior. When the new faith came on the scene, it "boldly identified the Deity of Vegetation, regarded as Life Principle, with the God of the Christian Faith."[25] Spanish missionaries would do much the same in the New World.

As is probably evident by now, nearly all the previous studies of the *saeta* have focused on its music. I would like to direct my attention to the poetry. The themes of the Passion and the Virgin's grief are found in Spanish verse beginning with Gonzalo de Berceo. In his work and in the *Cantigas de Santa María* of Alphonse the Wise, in Juan Ruiz and the other poets of the high Middle Ages, an optimistic tone of praise and miracles prevails. In the rare treatments of the Crucifixion, the serenity of the style often recalls the immobility of Romanesque sculpture. This is how Christ dies in Berceo:

> Inclinó la cabeza commo qui quier dormir,
> Rendió a Dios la alma e dessóse morir.[26]

These poets narrate episodes from the lives of Jesus and the Virgin with little lyrical expression. The octosyllable, the verse form that concerns us here, had been employed in the earliest Spanish poetry, yet it did not come to be used with any regularity until the late 1400s. About the same time, a new interest in the themes of the Passion developed in Spain. It therefore behooves us to look at this period for a double reason of content and form.

An important change in sensibility had taken place in European art during the fourteenth century. In music, the passage from *ars antiqua* to *ars nova,* with its greater expressiveness, rhythmic, harmonic, and melodic flexibility. In painting and sculpture, from an architectural to a pictorial style, from representations of the "remote and terrible God of the early Middle Ages to the Son of God made flesh, to the child at his mother's breast, to the tormented and blood-spattered man-God. . . ."[27] It was not until the following century that the new spirit would bear fruit in Spain. In religious poetry, narrative verse gave way to the lyric; the old four-line stanzas of alexandrines to the ballad, the *copla,* and the *villancico.* There were also signs of a religious ardor that adumbrated the great flourishing of Peninsular mysticism in the mid-1500s.

The new sensibility reached its plenitude in Spain during the period of the Catholic Kings. Two Franciscan poets, Iñigo de Mendoza and Ambrosio de Montesino, expressed new sentiments—themes of the Nativity and Passion—with a simple yet refined verse. The Carthusian monk Juan de Padilla applied the fine observation and realism of Flemish painting to the poetry of devotion. Diego de San Pedro meditated on the divine sacrifice with an intensity unknown until then in Spain, and the Comendador Román dared to include some of the apocryphal Christian legends in his didactic works. The new zeal was also communicated to profane authors who wrote poems in the religious style, *a lo divino.* On the stage, the graceful and pathetic "representations" and "lamentations" of Gómez Manrique, the dramatic primitivism of Lucas Fernández and Juan del Encina also corresponded to this mood.

The reasons for such an important change in sensibility should not detain us here, beyond saying that in the particular case of religious poetry, it was partly due to the Franciscan reform. The mendicant friars, following the example of their founder, exhorted listeners in everyday language to live their faith, to meditate upon the events of the Gospel, and to practice the "contemplation of Christ's humanity." The order's poet-friars condemned the elaborate and artificial style of classical oratory. The emotions they tried to evoke were "tenderness, fear, love, compassion, joy, and these feelings triumph over decorum. And respectfulness suffered damage in the process, as it sometimes still does in Spain on account of the 'intimacy with the divine' "[28] As respectfulness suffers damage in the *saeta*, we might add.[29]

What first comes to our notice in this poetry is an obsession with the Passion. Diego de San Pedro composed his *Pasión trovada;* the Comendador Román wrote his *Trovas de la gloriosa Pasión;* Mendoza, Montesino, and Juan de Padilla narrated episodes of Calvary and the Virgin's sorrows. Speaking of Mendoza's work, Angel Valbuena Prat says that in these poems, the emphatic pathos reminds one of the later Andalusian *saetas* or of the plasticity of the figures in Easter processions.[30] Here is how the Franciscan father describes the visage of the dying Christ:

> Con saliva blanqueada,
> con bofetadas bruñida,
> con tu sangre matizada,
> con lágrimas barnizada,
> con suspiros afligida,
> con escarnios denegrida,
> con semejanza terrible
> . . . .
> o vista descolorida
> . . . . [31]

The motif of Christ's paleness also appears in some *saetas:*

> Míralo, por allí viene
> el mejor de los nacidos,
> con una cruz en los hombros
> y el rostro descolorido.[32]

Mendoza wrote in double five-line stanzas of octosyllables, with a rhyme scheme (consonant) that is also used in the *saeta* (usually assonant):

a b a a b. The other major poet-friar of this period, Montesino, stressed the instruments of the Passion—the ropes that tied Christ to the column, the crown of thorns, and the nails. San Pedro dedicated fifty lines to the nailing on the cross alone. Padilla depicted the story of Calvary with a marvelous plasticity, having before him a reredos with scenes and figures from the Gospel; one thinks of the colored wooden carvings of Alonso Berruguete and Juan de Juni, slightly later in time. Román, whose lively imagination made up for a meager poetic gift, tells how the Roman soldiers had to stretch the Savior's arms with cords in order for them to reach the nail holes in the cross. This *saeta* relates a similar episode:

> Fueron tan mal señalados
> los tres barrenos crueles,
> que de sus pies consagrados
> tuvieron que atar cordeles
> y tirar para enclavarlo.[33]

Several other characteristics of this late medieval poetry recall the *saeta*. The Virgin's sorrow is treated as extensively as the Crucifixion. Popular legends mingle with the events of the New Testament; Mendoza wrote his *Coplas a la Verónica*. Christ's precious blood appears at every turn. Mary suffers when it drips to the ground, where it fertilizes the earth and is converted into flowers:

> los arroyos de la sangre
> arroyauan el terreno
> do la santa cruz estaua
> acuñada en el otero[34]
> . . . . ;
>
> Su corona tan penosa
> que viste llena de espinas,
> ya se le tornó preciosa
> corona real pomposa;
> sus espinas, clavellinas;
> sus puntas ensangrentadas
> son tornadas rosicler . . .
> . . . .

An anti-Jewish sentiment also appears:

> ¡O pueblo sin cortesía,
> vestido de escuras nieblas,
> donde en tanta osadía

que al señor de tu alegría
así lo fieres y quiebras![35]

Yet the author of this passage, Mendoza, was a convert, as was San Pedro. There is an immediacy and drama in this poetry that seems to look ahead to the *saeta*. The authors implore their readers, as the mendicant friars implored their listeners, to imagine the inexpressible physical pain of Jesus and the mental agony of the Virgin. Their intention is openly didactic. They incite the sinner with exhortations ("see," "contemplate," "look") to concentrate on the divine persons in order to reach a state of devotional meditation, much as the *saetero* urges his public to rivet its attention on the figures of the processions. Some scenes of this poetry are purely theatrical. In Padilla's *Retablo de la vida de Cristo*, we witness an encounter between Christ and his Mother on the road to Calvary. Choked with emotion, they are unable to speak to each other. Such scenes are reenacted in the Holy Week celebrations of some Spanish cities.[36] A famous *saeta* portrays this encounter:

En la caye 'e l'Amargura
Cristo a su Madre 'ncontró;
no se pudieron hablar
de sentimiento y dolor.[37]

The characters in the divine tragedy move, gesticulate, and speak: Jesus with Mary, Veronica, and Peter. The theatrical nature of the devotional poetry of the fifteenth century suggests that it may have grown out of religious drama, in which the Passion was also treated with pathos and tenderness—as in Gómez Manrique's *Lamentaciones fechas para Semana Santa* and Lucas Fernández' *Auto de la Pasión*. In the *Partidas* of Alphonse the Wise, we learn of the existence of a Spanish religious drama in the early Middle Ages. As in the rest of Europe, it was probably connected with the joyful celebrations of Christmas or the pathetic ceremonies of Holy Week. There was a tight relationship between religious poetry and drama in this period. For example, the following "desir" of the poet Juan Álvarez Gato echoes the Easter sequence:

Dy nobis, Maria,
que viste en la via.[38]

Speaking of Lucas Fernández' *Auto*, Valbuena Prat says significantly: "A popular enthusiasm accompanies the dramatic and bloody Christ . . . and this painful and realistic tableau reveals itself in *saetas*, blood and sculptured tears."[39]

Assuming that the *saeta* did acquire its lyrical form during the flourishing of popular religious poetry in fifteenth-century Spain, what was the song's fate between this period and its first known mention in print a hundred years later? A book written by the Franciscan Antonio de Ezcaray in 1691, and brought to light in modern times by Rodríguez Marín, reveals a possible key.[40] The book is entitled *Voces del Dolor;* though published in Seville, it refers to the author's experience in the New World. He and his confreres had the custom of singing *saetas* in the streets of Mexico City. Because of its importance, I reproduce this original passage in full:

> Mis hermanos, los reverendos padres del convento de nuestro padre San Francisco, todos los meses del año, el domingo de Cuerda por la tarde hacen misión, bajando la comunidad a andar el "Vía Crucis" con sogas y coronas de espinas, y entre paso y paso cantan saetas, y después hay sermón.

A few years later, at the beginning of the eighteenth century, some loose sheets with a bombastic title appeared: "Saetas espirituales que los padres predicadores de la religión seráfica de nuestro padre San Francisco van cantando por las calles en las misiones que hacen por toda España con orden de Su Santidad." Is it only a coincidence that two of the earliest known mentions of these songs refer to Franciscan friars? If not, we might ask ourselves why members of the order in other countries were not singing *saetas* at the same time.[41] The answer must be that the form and spirit of these songs grew out of peculiarly Spanish circumstances. The devotional poetry in the Peninsula during the reign of the Catholic Kings, when the *saeta* probably began to acquire its lyrical character, had no exact parallel in other parts of Europe. Though not exclusively Andalusian, the primitive *saeta* must have been specifically Spanish. The missionaries of the Franciscan Order could have disseminated it throughout the Peninsula and the Americas. With the passing of time, the song might have outgrown the monastic mold, as it had previously outgrown the narrow bounds of liturgy and sacred drama. Its language and tone would thus have become more popular, less didactic. From a song of edification, it would have evolved into a "deeper and more passionate expression of individual feeling."[42]

The existence of a popular religious poetry might seem contradictory during the period of the Counter-Reformation, when a highly refined mysticism was thriving. Saint John of the Cross was never a poet of the masses, for example. But beneath his works and those of Saint Ignatius of Loyola, Saint Teresa, and Luis de Granada, a stream of popular poetry flows, which sprang directly from the previous centuries. The traditional poetry of the Middle Ages prolonged itself throughout the Golden Age. The beautiful Renaissance song collections, religious and profane, formed a bridge between late medieval verse in Spain and that of the seventeenth and eighteenth centuries: the *Cancionero espiritual* (1549), the *Cancionero de Nuestra Señora* (1591), and the famous *Cancionero musical de los siglos XV y XVI*, to mention only a few. Most of the traditional religious poetry of the Golden Age is basically medieval in language and themes.

After its secularization and expansion, the most important phase in this hypothetical development of the *saeta* would have been its assimilation of Andalusian music during the great period of *cante jondo* in the mid-nineteenth century. But the verses remain essentially the same. At any rate, the *saeta* had assumed a definitive character by the late 1800s.

For the time being then, we can define the *saeta* as a survival of an ancient seasonal rite of the Mediterranean world, later Christianized, which may have taken on its poetic form in the liturgy of the Middle Ages or more probably in the traditional religious verse of fifteenth-century Spain; spread throughout the Spanish empire by Franciscan friars, it eventually became secularized and acquired a typical musical character in Andalusia during the mid-1800s under the influence of *cante jondo*. It is possible that the coexistence of Moors and Jews in Spain over a long period left some traces on the form, but these are extremely hard to isolate and it is unlikely that they were decisive. All we can say with certainty is that the music of the *saeta* sounds more "Oriental" than its poetry.

"POEMA DE LA SAETA"

García Lorca was not highly versed in the history of the *saeta:* nearly all the theories discussed above have been developed since his death. Yet he revealed the ancient roots of this song with a remarkable poetic intuition. In his "Poema de la saeta," he seems to express the discoveries of musicologists and critics in a lyrical form.

Lorca's poem is divided into eight sections and it constitutes one of the major parts of his *Poema del cante jondo* (I:177-86). Before examining its symbolic meaning, we should look at the poem on a literal level. The first section, "Arqueros," creates the air of mystery and expectation before Holy Week in Seville. From the towns in the surrounding countryside, pilgrims flock to the capital. Among them are the "archers" or singers of *saetas*, who will shoot their arrowlike songs into the night:

> Los arqueros oscuros
> a Sevilla se acercan.
>
> Guadalquivir abierto.
>
> Anchos sombreros grises,
> largas capas lentas.
>
> ¡Ay, Guadalquivir!
>
> Vienen de los remotos
> países de la pena.
>
> Guadalquivir abierto.
>
> Y van a un laberinto.
> Amor, cristal y piedra.
>
> ¡Ay, Guadalquivir!

The scene is appropriately nocturnal, as in flamenco verse and the *saeta* in particular. This initial poem abounds with somber suggestions. The dark pilgrims wear gray, wide-brimmed hats and flowing capes. They come from remote lands of sorrow to the labyrinth of the city's winding streets and alleys. In contrast to these forebodings, the waters of the great Guadalquivir River—giving Seville her life, fertility, and beauty—run freely to the sea. This is the first mention of water in the "Poema de la saeta." The element will recur under various forms throughout the poem.

The second section, "Noche," sets the scene for the action. We are no longer on the wide river plain, but inside the city. The time is probably very early on Good Friday morning, just before dawn.

> Cirio, candil,
> farol y luciérnaga.
>
> La constelación
> de la saeta.
>
> Ventanitas de oro
> tiemblan,

> y en la aurora se mecen
> cruces superpuestas.
>
> Cirio, candil,
> farol y luciérnaga.

This is not the somber light of tragedy, introduced in the previous fragment. It is rather a quaint light, perhaps too much so: the thin wax candles on the floats or *pasos*, iron lamps on street corners, the flicker of fireflies. The litters seem to tremble on the shoulders of penitents and the crosses carried by the members of the brotherhoods stir in the dawn air. The plasticity of the description is as remarkable as that of the wooden images in this kind of procession.

The third section, "Seville," is a paean to this marvelous city. Lorca confronts it with Cordova.

> Sevilla es una torre
> llena de arqueros finos.
>
> Sevilla para herir,
> Córdoba para morir.
>
> Una ciudad que acecha
> largos ritmos,
> y los enrosca
> como laberintos.
> Como tallos de parra
> encendidos.
>
> ¡Sevilla para herir!
>
> Bajo el arco del cielo,
> sobre su llano limpio,
> dispara la constante
> saeta de su río.
>
> ¡Córdoba para morir!
>
> Y loca de horizonte,
> mezcla en su vino,
> lo amargo de Don Juan
> y lo perfecto de Dionisio.
>
> Sevilla para herir.
> ¡Siempre Sevilla para herir!

Seville wounds the sensibility with her refined, passionate grace, and with the figurative arrows of her *saetas*. Cordova, on the other hand, is a place for concentration and death. In the poet's own words, it is the "most melancholy city of Andalusia" (I:1024), the very opposite of Seville. The tower of the latter's Cathedral, the Giralda, embodies her spirit: solid and elegant, sober and ornate. She twists the long, free rhythms of her *saetas* into delicate arabesques, like labyrinths or flaming vineshoots. The Guadalquivir itself resembles a song and an arrow, shot across a flat expanse of alluvial plain. In her soul, Seville combines a Christian awareness of sin—the legend of Don Juan—with a classical sense of beauty—Dionysus.

Now that the stage and scenery have been set, the drama begins. The remaining sections evoke the *saeta* itself; its eruption into the sky will be the culmination of the poem. In "Procesión," Lorca describes the approach of a float or *paso*. First come the penitents with their robes and pointed hoods, "weird unicorns." Then the wooden figure of the crucified Christ.

> Por la calleja vienen
> extraños unicornios.
> ¿De qué campo,
> de qué bosque mitológico?
> Más cerca,
> ya parecen astrónomos.
> Fantásticos Merlines
> y el Ecce Homo,
> Durandarte encantado,
> Orlando furioso.

The penitents look like wise men or magicians out of the Middle Ages, and Jesus recalls the knights-errant, Roland and Durandarte. This fragment seems to evoke the Grail romances, in which the "central figure is either a dead knight on a bier . . . or a wounded king on a litter."[43] In the "mythological forest" on the one hand, and the astronomers-Merlins-knights on the other, we recognize the two faces of Easter and the *saeta:* classical and medieval, Greco-Roman and Gothic.

In this Lorcan chiaroscuro, a bright emblem of popular faith now illuminates the darkness of the streets where the silent penitents have just passed. The Virgin's "Paso," with its hundreds of white candles, is like a boat of light floating down the street to the sea.

> Virgen con miriñaque,
> virgen de la Soledad,

abierta   como   un   in-
menso
tulipán.
En tu barco de luces
vas
por la alta marea
de la ciudad,
entre saetas turbias
y estrellas de cristal.
Virgen con miriñaque,
tú vas
por el río de la calle
¡hasta el mar!

Lorca seems to have been fascinated by the unrestrained Baroque imagination of popular Andalusian decoration: saints covered with lace and
trinkets, virgins in embroidered mantels, puppet theaters with little cur-
tains and arabesques.[44] The sensuality of this lyric suggests a kind of
luscious paganism—lights, crinoline, open tulip. An undercurrent of
mystery and the "turbid" *saetas* prepare for the tragedy to follow.

"Saeta" is the summit of the poem. In contrast to the other fragments,
which evoke an atmosphere, it approximates an actual *saeta*.

Cristo moreno
pasa
de lirio de Judea
a clavel de España.

¡Miradlo por dónde viene!

De España.
Cielo limpio y oscuro,
tierra tostada,
y cauces donde corre
muy lenta el agua.
Cristo moreno,
con las guedejas quemadas,
los pómulos salientes
y las pupilas blancas.

¡Miradlo por dónde va!

The last four verses before the final refrain could be considered an independent *saeta*. In them we see the usual irregular meter and assonance in
the even lines, and the common motif of Christ's pale complexion. But

Lorca knew better than to imitate popular poetry, as we learned in his lecture on *cante jondo*. These verses are too objective and detached to be a real *saeta*. They are traced and limited in the most precise manner, as if the poet were afraid of falling into the slightest sentimentality. They embody the special character of Spanish art discussed by Lorca in one of his lectures: "the beauty of Spain is not serene, sweet, restful, but ardent, scorched, excessive" (I:1046).

The last two sections of "Poema de la saeta" form the aftermath. In "Balcón," the poet explores the psychology of a woman who sings *saetas*. Lola is one of the marginal figures to whom Lorca was endeared, like the crazy children and beggars who occasionally appear in his work.[45] From her flower-laden balcony, she seems to find release from her anguish by singing *saetas*. From below, men and young boys watch her with lusty eyes.

> La Lola
> canta saetas.
> Los toreritos
> la rodean,
> y el barberillo
> desde su puerta,
> sigue los ritmos
> con la cabeza.
> Entre la albahaca
> y la hierbabuena
> la Lola canta
> saetas.
> La Lola aquella,
> que se miraba
> tanto en la alberca.

The stagnant water of the pool in which Lola looks at her reflection contrasts with the healthy running water of rivers. She must harbor a great despair and perhaps she feels the temptation of suicide. According to tradition, the best singers of *saetas* used to be anonymous beggars, blind men or women, and lunatics—before the professionalism of our times. Lola belongs to this fringe of society. She is portrayed in more detail in another poem of Lorca's book, "Dos muchachas" (I:199). Even more than in "Balcón," the poet juxtaposes the elements that go to make up a love lyric—flowering orange trees, sunshine, running water, birds—with a perverse reality—a woman who sadly seeks to heal her lost illusions in a banal liaison with young boys. The important point for us is that Lorca has revealed how the *saeta* may be as much an expression of the singer's anxiety as of religious devotion.

In the last part of the "Poema de la saeta," called "Madrugada," the moon cuts through the clouds, dew falls, dawn arrives, and the mystery has ended.

> Pero como el amor
> los saeteros
> están ciegos.
>
> Sobre la noche verde,
> las saetas
> dejan rastros de lirio
> caliente.
>
> La quilla de la luna
> rompe nubes moradas
> y las aljabas
> se llenan de rocío.
>
> ¡Ay, pero como el amor
> los saeteros
> están ciegos!

We have come full circle: the blind *saeteros* are the same "dark archers" who approached Seville in the first section of the poem. They will now return to their remote lands, their quivers empty of arrows. The traces of their songs remain in the sky like burning flowers. The beauty of the *saeta* is that of Spain as described by Lorca: "blind from its own splendor, it beats its head against the walls" (I:1046). The time is Easter, but for this unredeemable land and the men who inhabit it, there is no suggestion of salvation.

The "Poema de la saeta" is a kind of dramatic miniature, progressing in time from night to dawn, evoking the scenery—city, street, balcony where the action transpires—processions and the culminating *saeta*. Everything interlocks; nothing is independent except the emotion of each fragment. Beneath this exterior flows the symbolic meaning of the poem, the obscure drama of light and darkness, religion and myth, tragedy and ecstasy, life and death.

The pilgrims come to Seville from faraway countries of sorrow, as the *saeta* rises from remote lands and cultures and from a deep well of suffering. The pilgrims enter a labyrinth of tortuous streets and alleys, a maze of rites and legend. Lorca also compares the *saeta* to a labyrinth and to a grapevine, thus expressing the intricacy and irregularity of its melodies and rhythms. The grapevine introduces the motif of wine, which is a fermentation of the "bitterness of Don Juan" and the "perfection of Dionysus," the Bacchus of the Romans. In a poem about Easter, the presence of wine inevitably must be associated with the blood of Christ and the sacrifice of the Mass. The legend of Don Juan with its bitter moral—God will punish man's sins if he does not repent before death—is also part of the Catholic element in the poem. In the Andalusian's soul, there is a struggle between Christian and pagan forces: the mood of repentance so proper to Good Friday, and the simultaneous, orgiastic exaltation of the flesh. Don Juan and Dionysus represent the two poles.

As if these suggestions were not enough, the poet asks from what "mythological forest" these strange rites come. The penitents recall unicorns   in their pointed dunce caps; this fabulous animal was a traditional symbol of the fertility and abundance of the earth. For her part, the Virgen de la Soledad resembles an immense, open tulip. The choice of this flower is not fortuitous: it is the first to blossom in spring. The Virgin is surrounded by images of water. She goes on her boat of candles over the tide of the city, down the river of the street to the sea. These are the clear, fecundating waters of the Guadalquivir, in contrast to the turbid, slow-moving waters of the hinterland, or the pool in which Lola discovered the fascination of death. Nevertheless, the waters of the river run to the sea, as human life runs toward death. Water symbolism formed an important part in ancient seasonal rites and in the Grail romances.[46]

Like his Mother, the figure of Christ is also related to flowers. From the "lily of Judea" he has become the "carnation of Spain." These flowers, as we have seen, recur over and over in the *saeta*. They suggest Christ's blood—the carnation—against his pale skin. The carnation may also be an emblem of passion and love, the lily an emblem of pain and suffering.[47] Another possibility is that the lily is purple instead of white; in Andalusia, it may be a synonym for black and blue marks on the skin. The following is an example of a *saeta* in which this flower is used in such a sense, side by side with the carnation:

> En el portal de Belén
> nació un clavel encarnado

que, por redimir al mundo,
se ha vuelto lirio morado.[48]

In the "Poema de la saeta," Lorca seems to have intuited the mythic roots of this song and its possible genesis in a seasonal rite of the pagan world. The pattern of allusions to labyrinths, flowers, blood, water, ancient legends, and mythological figures is probably too pervasive to be the result of mere chance. The crucified Christ is borne across the city like an adored phallus. Like other Lorcan heroes—Sánchez Mejías, Antoñito el Camborio—he resembles a sacrificial pagan god. The poet has also seen the essentially medieval quality of this ancient rite: its intimate, liturgical drama, the penitents with their evocations of magic and superstition, the Christian ideas of sin and repentance. The image of Christ recalls a knight-errant in addition to a classical deity. Like Easter and the *saeta*, the romances of chivalry, with their central motif of the Holy Grail, also represent a cycle of spiritual death and regeneration. In fact the Grail legend offers another example of how an ancient ritual became Christianized during the Middle Ages.

In the language of literary criticism, myth is often considered to stand at the opposite pole from history and other forms of logos. Thus the mythic expresses the intuitive concrete, in contrast to the rational abstract. In Lorca's "Poema de la saeta," we witness a rare example of how art can fuse history and myth.

IV. The Tragic Myth

Chapter Eight

Conclusion

Music formed an intimate part of García Lorca's life and work. His charisma as an individual and a poet was perhaps due above all to a basic musical feeling, attested to by those who knew him. Lorca carried the songs of his land in the blood, as if by a millennial inheritance. Vicente Aleixandre, in his Prologue to the poet's collected works, compares him to an old, fabulous, and mythic *cantaor*, as wise, eternal, and rooted in the earth as a mountain (II:IX). From his native soil Lorca imbibed the musical grace and sense of tragedy that give his work its unmistakable accent. Yet he was not a regional poet. He considered himself to be first a brother of all men, then a Spaniard, finally an Andalusian and Granadine. He may have been the most Spanish of writers; he is the only modern poet of his country with a worldwide reputation. His poetry sounds a unique melody, but one that counterpoints the anguish of our century. What in other artists is the product of historical circumstances, or the spirit of the times, in Lorca is an attachment to the earth and its ancient voices. The most profound of these voices make up the music known as *cante jondo*.

Lorca rarely tried to imitate the poetry of this music. There are echoes of traditional songs in his early plays, and especially in his Andalusian verse—*Poema del cante jondo*, *Romancero gitano*, *Llanto por Ignacio Sánchez Mejías*, and *Diván del Tamarit*. In these works, as well as in his major tragedies and the *Poeta en Nueva York*, the indirect resonances of *cante jondo* are more subtle and elusive, yet far more important: a geographic and temporal precision, a kind of visceral suffering, an atmosphere of extremes, an oscillation between plenitude and death, and finally, a dramatic attitude, ecstatic tone, and graphic imagery whose closest model would probably be the *saeta*.

The music Lorca heard as a child on the Granadine *vega* never ceased to ring in his mind. He submerged himself in the traditional songs of his land, absorbing the genius of the people and their modes of expression.

His sources merely supplied the component parts of his work; the total atmosphere belongs to him alone. None of the typical elements of *cante jondo* is missing from his verse: song, dance, guitar, *pena*, Andalusia, gypsy. Stylized and transfigured to the plane of poetry, they serve as stepping stones to a highly original creation. Daniel Devoto refers to the poet's "decisive step from the national—almost the regional—a root and trampoline, to the universal, for everyone and for all time."[1] Lorca absorbed the traditional songs of Andalusia so thoroughly that they merged with his own inspiration, giving birth to a new and superior world of poetry.

Like the Hispano-Arabic lyricists and the popular poet, Lorca found the raw material for his art in the world around him, rather than in an inner realm of thought and feeling. Thus his verse abounds with local and temporal elements. Concrete things and the sensations they provoke expand into a world of cosmic dimensions—scent, light, and emotion turned to a music full of distance and memory. The tangible allusions to Andalusian objects, people, and songs become part of a new whole, unlimited in time or space. Lorca might conceivably have taken a different road, constructing a private world of image and revery in the recesses of his being. This was the way of Juan Ramón Jiménez. But the poet of the *Llanto* chose another path, at once easier and more arduous. He reached the domain of beauty and myth through a transcendent vision of a specific reality. In this sense he remained faithful to *duende* and the spirit of the land.

Thus Lorca, like the anonymous poets of *cante jondo*, drew his inspiration from a concrete reality. His art could be called more physical than spiritual; in it the will prevails over reason in a premoral and subintellectual world. The categories of time, space, substance, and form are sometimes operative, but they are frequently suspended too. As in ancient myth, objective events and subjective states bear a peculiar relation to one another. Lorca and the *cantaor* observe the cosmos in a way comparable to that of primitive man: the coincidence of events becomes more important than their sequence according to the law of causality. Natural phenomena, such as the appearance of the moon, may influence human destiny—usually in a negative manner. Life flowers in images, light, and fables yet it is constantly imperiled by mysterious forces.

We find in Lorca and *cante jondo* a return to the elementary which is one of the marks of a world in revolt against itself. Extremism, violence, and blood betray a tendency to rebellion which has its origins in the darkest places of the mind. The ultimate consequences of Lorca's creation, if extended to the real world, would be no less than revolutionary in both a political and a psychological sense. The poet stands on the side of instinct, freedom, and the oppressed members of society, whether they be children, women, blacks, or gypsies. The forces that brought about his death were appropriately those of reaction, yet Lorca, like the *cantaor*, never attempted to transpose his art onto a political, social, or philosophic plane. *Duende* represents an end in itself and offers no solutions in a world fatally marked by suffering.

For Lorca, his native land came to signify a region saved from the worst abstraction and materialism, where an ancient culture had firm roots, where communal art forms like bullfighting and *cante jondo* could flourish, and where the brave man still commanded respect. In his work, almost unique in modern poetry, a world remains of which man is the sole master. The characters of his plays, the anonymous figures of his poetry, the gypsies and Sánchez Mejías confront death, fate, and injustice with a clear dignity. In a contest in which they are conquered from the outset, they refuse to accept defeat. Bravery, duty, love, and risk are the tributes man pays to his honor in this unequal campaign. It is a matter of being faithful to the rule of battle. This thought may suffice to sustain a mind such as Seneca's. It has supported whole cultures, in particular the Andalusian. If Lorca comes to be recognized as something more than an exotic magician of the word, his message must reside in this deep sense of human suffering and dignity: fruit of a racial inheritance and a personal intuition.

In the poet's work and in *cante jondo*, the subject matter and related emotions tend to fall into a characteristic pattern of meaning. Though happiness and optimism are not entirely absent, this basic pattern discloses what could be called a tragic vision. As described by Northrop Frye, the archetype of the tragic plot or myth in literature might illuminate Lorca's poetry in relation to *cante jondo*.[2] In general, the human world of the tragic myth is represented as a tyranny or anarchy, symbolized by the isolated hero. The animal world is seen in terms of wild rather than domesticated creatures—beasts, birds of prey, serpents. The vegetable world appears as a forest or wilderness. Finally, the mineral world condenses in stones and ruins.

We do not have to stretch our imagination to realize the significance of such a pattern for our subject. Of course the scheme is highly over-simplified. Only the specific context of each work will yield the meaning of its images and symbols. The lyrical climate of the Andalusian song, in its most basic forms, portrays a wasteland peopled by solitary men. In the *Poema del cante jondo*, lonely, anonymous gypsies plod to their unhappy end amid an equally sterile landscape. In the *Romancero gitano*, man also finds himself in a hostile atmosphere; the gypsies embody the human lot. In both *cante jondo* and the works of Lorca, the injustice of society is understood a priori; the rich and the powerful govern without compassion or appeal. The individual has nothing to guide him but his own instincts; the result is an anarchy of opposing wills. There is little more than fleeting contact between men, virtually no feeling of community.

The bestiaries of the *cantaor* and the poet also show a tendency toward chaos and violence. The most typical animals in each case are probably the bull, birds of prey, and snakes. In Lorca, even such innocent creatures as butterflies and doves are metamorphosed into obscure omens. Other elements of his animal kingdom include nightingales, crocodiles, spiders, ants, worms, and flies. The vegetable kingdom is hardly more encouraging. In the Andalusian song, flowers may be emblems of sensual beauty or passion in the midst of a barren landscape. In Lorca, the negative aspects of flowers predominate: the deathly odor of spikenards, the white sterility of camellias, the bloody color of carnations, the acidity of lemons, the bitterness of olives and oleanders. Moreover, a kind of primal vegetation—composed of seaweed, moss, fungus, and herbs—threatens to overgrow the ruins left by life and civilization. Both *cante jondo* and Lorca's poetry revolve around the declining phase of the natural, organic, and human cycles, suggested by images of twilight and darkness, autumn and winter, decay and death. This is the scenario for tragedy and elegy in literature—for myths of fall, the dying god, violent death, and sacrifice. The *Llanto*, with the solitary hero's quest for life against the dark powers embodied by the bull, acted out upon a symbolic landscape, may be one of the most consistent and profound expressions of the tragic myth in modern poetry.

Thus myth and the tragic vision are the unifying forces between Lorca's work and *cante jondo*. In the traditional Andalusian song, anguish and suffering may manifest themselves through the words of the poetry, but chiefly through the suggestions of the music. The tragic sense in Lorca also transcends the verse, since it derives from a feeling too vast, complex, and indefinable to be contained in words alone. Like Nietzsche, the Granadine poet sought the musical essence of tragedy. Perhaps the philosopher's Dionysian spirit could be fruitfully compared to *duende* in this respect. The Greek god of wine and intoxication was also the patron of wild music, orgy, and the dancing throng. In one of his lectures, Lorca said that Nietzsche's Dionysian spirit had migrated directly from Greece to Andalusia, to the dancing girls of Cadiz and the *siguiriya* of Silverio.[3] The ritual importance of wine, a current of sexual desire, the trance in which men discovered their subconscious selves and the primordial unity of nature— these are some of the elements common to the ancient mysteries and the performance of *cante jondo* under the inspiration of *duende*.

Nietzsche believed that tragedy constituted a visible symbolization of music, a verbal expression of Dionysian dreams and emotions. He made the value of art depend not upon the formal excellence of the work itself, but upon the tension in the soul of the artist who produced it, or upon the process—strenuous or facile—by which the spectator apprehended it. In this sense, he anticipated Lorca's valuation of art according to *duende*. For the poet and the Andalusian singer, intensity is more important than esthetic perfection. Thus the importance they grant to extreme situations, and Lorca's preference for passionate artists over more accomplished masters: for Paganini over Brahms, Saint John of the Cross over Garcilaso, El Greco over Velázquez. "Each step climbed by a man in his tower of perfection, by an artist as Nietzsche would say, must be made at the expense of a struggle with his *duende*" (I:1069).

In Lorca and *cante jondo* we sense a strife between the artist and his inspiration or *duende*. The singer's emotion is so overbearing that it breaks the limits of form. In the poet, feeling may be more controlled, but the impulse is the same. In both, the taste of mortality, the overflow of pathos, and the dwelling on pain are out of proportion to their possible causes. Death lurks in the shadows, then swallows man in a climate of mysterious signs and premonitions. The odds are weighed against human life; a benevolent providence does not watch over men. The good are not rewarded, crime goes unpunished. In this terrifying universe, there is no quarter from the hounds of destiny, no margin for compromise.

Yet in the middle of this labyrinth, a light glimmers. Because he has touched the depth of human anguish, the artist—poet or *cantaor*—has earned the right to sing. The world may be evil, but the intensity of suffering has let us glimpse, even for a hallowed moment, the realm where life mingles with death and man embraces his fate with dignity and joy. As in tragedy, tears and pain have purged the spirit. After the terror of the night the new and ancient dawn returns to illumine the sorrowing earth. In the silence of this crucial Lorcan hour, at the crossroads of light and darkness, the notes of a distant, ageless song begin to reach our ears.

Notes

Chapter 1

1. This lecture was presented on the night of February 19 in the Centro Artístico y Literario of Granada and reprinted under the title "El cante jondo—Primitivo canto andaluz." Federico García Lorca, *Obras completas,* 18th ed. (Madrid: Aguilar, 1974), I: 973-94. All references to Lorca's work (in both text and notes) are to this edition.

2. This and all other translations are mine (I: 975).

3. *Siguiriya* of course represents the gypsy and popular Andalusian pronunciation of *seguidilla.* The flamenco form should be distinguished from the Castilian *seguidilla* in both its verse and its music.

4. According to John A. Crow, the gypsies entered Spain across the Pyrenees in 1440; there is proof of their being in Barcelona in some numbers by 1447. See *Spain: The Root and the Flower* (New York: Harper and Row, 1963), pp. 21, 73.

5. "Arquitectura del cante jondo," delivered in the Salón Imperial of Seville on March 30. A summary of the lecture appears in *Obras completas* (I: 995-1000).

6. Lorca had probably read a recent article that caused some stir in Spanish intellectual circles, " 'Cante jondo' y cantares sinagogales," by Medina Azara (a pseudonym of Máximo José Kahn). The article appeared in *Revista de Occidente,* 8 (October 1930), 53-84. I will discuss it in Chapter 7.

7. *El cante jondo: Canto primitivo andaluz* (Granada: Editorial Urania, 1922). The poet may have known Falla's work before it was published.

8. Perhaps the only other musicologist to make a positive contribution to our general technical knowledge has been Manuel García Matos. See especially his article, "Cante flamenco: Algunos de sus presuntos orígenes," *Anuario Musical,* 5 (1950), 97-124. Arcadio de Larrea and Adolfo Salazar have studied some of the individual forms. The best nontechnical treatment is probably Ricardo Molina and Antonio Mairena, *Mundo y formas del cante flamenco* (Madrid: Revista de Occidente, 1963). For a general treatment in English, see Gilbert Chase, *The Music of Spain* (1941; rpt. New York: Dover, 1959).

9. Molina and Mairena, *Mundo y formas,* pp. 27ff. I will follow these authors in the historical summary below.

10. *El cancionero de Abén Guzmán: Discursos leídos ante la Real Academia Española* (Madrid: Imprenta Ibérica, 1912).

11. See Fernando Quiñones, "Los cafés de cante," *La Estafeta Literaria,* No.

456 (15 November 1970), pp. 16-20. This issue of the magazine is devoted to Lorca and *cante jondo.*

12. See the entry "flamenco" in Joan Corominas, *Breve diccionario etimológico de la lengua castellana* (Madrid: Gredos, 1967).

13. This is true especially in the case of the *saeta.* See Chapter 7, below.

14. Molina and Mairena, *Mundo y formas,* pp. 74-75.

15. But see entry "duende" in Corominas, *Breve diccionario etimológico,* and Yakov Malkiel, *Estudios hispánicos: Homenaje a Archer M. Huntington* (Wellesley, Mass.: Wellesley College, 1952), pp. 361-92.

16. Christoph Eich, *Federico García Lorca: Poeta de la intensidad* (Madrid: Gredos, 1970), p. 126. Eich's treatment of *duende* is helpful for understanding this concept in Lorca.

17. For example: "Recordad el caso de la flamenquísima y enduendada Santa Teresa . . ." (I: 1076).

18. Dámaso Alonso, *Poetas españoles contemporáneos* (Madrid: Gredos, 1958), pp. 271-80.

19. Eich, *Federico García Lorca,* pp. 40-41.

Chapter 2

1. José Mora Guarnido, *Federico García Lorca y su mundo* (Buenos Aires: Losada, 1958), p. 160. The most complete treatment of the competition and the composer's role in it is Eduardo Molina Fajardo's *Manuel de Falla y el cante jondo* (Granada: Universidad de Granada, 1962).

2. Quoted in Anselmo González Climent, *Flamencología: Toros, cante y baile* (Madrid: Escelicer, 1964), p. 274.

3. Walter Starkie, "Cante Jondo, Flamenco and the Guitar," *Guitar Review,* No. 20 (1956), p. 4.

4. Falla, "Il canto primitivo andaluso," *La Rassegna Musicale,* No. 10 (October 1938), p. 358.

5. Molina and Mairena, *Mundo y formas,* pp. 69ff.

6. Rafael Lafuente, *Los gitanos, el flamenco y los flamencos* (Barcelona: Barna, 1955), p. 120.

7. See the discussion of this city in Chapter 5, below.

8. Mora Guarnido, *Federico García Lorca,* p. 162.

Chapter 3

1. Daniel Devoto, "Notas sobre el elemento tradicional en la obra de García Lorca," *Filología,* No. 1 (May-August 1949), p. 293.

2. Emphasis in the quotation is mine.

3. Hipólito Rossy, *Teoría del cante jondo* (Barcelona: Credsa, 1966), p. 256.

4. Ricardo Molina, *Cante flamenco* (Madrid: Taurus, 1965), p. 136. This is not the same work as the author's *Mundo y formas del cante flamenco,* written in collaboration with the singer Antonio Mairena and cited in the first two chapters.

5. Molina, *Cante flamenco*, p. 141.

6. Molina, *Cante flamenco*, p. 91.

7. The *saeta* will be discussed extensively in Chapter 7 where some of the comparisons made here will come into better focus. Here, it is sufficient to say that the *saeta* is a religious song in the style of *cante jondo,* sung during Spanish Easter processions, and characterized by a dramatic structure, flower symbolism, an ecstatic tone, and clear, realistic imagery describing Christ's Passion.

8. Agustín Aguilar y Tejera, *Saetas populares* (Madrid: Compañía Ibero-Americana de Publicaciones, n.d.), no. 782.

9. Carlos Ramos-Gil, *Claves líricas de García Lorca: Ensayos sobre la expresión y los climas poéticos lorquianos* (Madrid: Aguilar, 1967), p. 273.

10. Eich, *Federico García Lorca,* p. 119.

11. Gino L. Rizzo, "Poesía de Federico García Lorca y poesía popular," *Clavileño,* No. 36 (November-December 1955), pp. 44-51.

12. Antonio Machado y Álvarez, *Cantes flamencos* (1881; rpt. Buenos Aires: Espasa Calpe, 1947), p. 28. This is one of the earliest and best collections of flamenco verse.

13. Domingo Manfredi Cano, *Geografía del cante jondo* (Madrid: Grifón, 1955), p. 169.

14. This collective bias is another "mythic" aspect of Lorca's work, to be developed in part III.

15. Tomás Andrade de Silva, "Sobre los orígenes de treinta y tres cantes," *Antología del cante flamenco* (Madrid: Hispavox, 1958), p. 84. The author's article serves as an introduction to this recorded anthology.

16. Before leaving this subject, I should note in passing that Lorca's sketches reveal another aspect of his visceral imagery. Even more than drama, the mute, objective medium of drawing offered him an impersonal vehicle for expressing his feelings. In his sketches, mental or emotional suffering is portrayed through physical pain or even mutilation of the body (see especially "Manos cortadas" and "Muerte," [I:1251, 1261]).

17. "In the volume's fifty-one poems, twenty-two variations on the idea of death can be counted." Alfredo de la Guardia, *García Lorca: Persona y creación* (Buenos Aires: Sur, 1949), p. 187.

18. Juan López-Morillas, "Lyrical Primitivism: García Lorca's *Romancero gitano,* " in *Lorca: A Collection of Critical Essays,* ed. Manuel Durán (Englewood Cliffs, N.J.: Prentice-Hall, 1962), pp. 136-37.

Chapter 4

1. "Cantares," Federico Carlos Sainz de Robles, *Historia y antología de la poesía española* (Madrid: Aguilar, 1955), p. 1218.

2. Antonio Machado y Álvarez, *Cantes flamencos,* pp. 84, 77.

3. Andrade de Silva, "Sobre los orígenes de treinta y tres cantes," *Antología del cante flamenco,* p. 63.

4. From a reading of his own work by the poet.

5. Mora Guarnido, *Federico García Lorca y su mundo,* p. 75.
6. Claude Couffon, *Granada y García Lorca* (Buenos Aires: Losada, 1967), pp. 24-25.
7. John A. Crow, *Federico García Lorca* (Los Angeles: University of California Press, 1945), p. 3.
8. See Chapter 5, below.
9. Sand often signifies death and sterility in Lorca's poetry. See Ramos-Gil, *Claves líricas,* pp. 139-40.
10. He also wrote a review of a concert given by this musician in Granada in May of 1920, discussed below.
11. The general atmosphere and the presence of nightingales suggest a violent death.
12. As in this example from Rossy, *Teoría del cante jondo,* pp. 259-60.

—¿Dónde vas, bella judía
tan compuesta y a deshora?
—Voy en busca de Rebeco
que espera en la sinagoga.

13. One music and art critic, Frederic V. Grunfeld, says the guitar in Goya is the symbol of a "passionate and disordered Spain." *The Art and Times of the Guitar: An Illustrated History of Guitars and Guitarists* (New York: Macmillan, 1970), pp. 139-40.
14. In the last poem, sand is once again a correlative of death.
15. *The Gypsies* (Baltimore: Penguin, 1969), p. 231.
16. "Vida y obra," *Federico García Lorca (1898-1936): Vida y Obra. Bibliografía. Antología. Obras inéditas. Música popular.* (New York: Hispanic Institute, 1941), p. 33.
17. Eich, *Federico García Lorca,* pp. 76-78.
18. *La poesía mítica de Federico García Lorca* (Madrid: Gredos, 1970), pp. 34ff.
19. See Chapter 6, below.
20. Edwin Honig, "Triumph of Sensual Reality—Mature Verse," in *Lorca* (ed. Durán), p. 96.
21. *De Baudelaire au surréalisme* (Paris: José Corti, 1966), p. 77.
22. As in Lorca's "Canto de la miel" (I:38).
23. "Homenaje, pour le tombeau de Debussy" (1926).
24. Falla said the guitar has "always held a favorite place in the resonant rooms of the Hispanic home." Prologue to Emilio Pujol's *Escuela razonada de la guitarra* (Buenos Aires: Ricordi Americana, 1956), p. 5. Falla wrote the Prologue in December 1933.
25. See next chapter.
26. "Cante Jondo, Flamenco and the Guitar," p. 6.
27. In *Mariana Pineda,* the ballad describing the *corrida* in Ronda is more descriptive than symbolic. It will not concern me here.
28. "Lyrical Primitivism," p. 136.
29. Lafuente, *Los gitanos,* p. 59.
30. J. Caro Baroja, *Los pueblos de España: Ensayo de etnología* (Barcelona:

Barna, 1946), p. 136. In his lecture on *duende,* Lorca reveals an awareness of this tradition in the Peninsula which he associates with the ancient cult of the bull in Crete (I:1071).

31. J. F. Cirre, "El caballo y el toro en la poesía de García Lorca," *Cuadernos Americanos,* No. 6 (November-December 1952), pp. 243, 245. The author notes that the "forgotten religions of Tartessos" reflourish in the rite of bullfighting.

Chapter 5

1. Roy Campbell, *Lorca* (London, New Haven: Yale University Press, 1952), p. 8.
2. *La poesía mítica,* p. 11.
3. From a letter to Jorge Zalamea (II:1233).
4. *Federico García Lorca,* p. 73.
5. *Teoría de Andalucía y otros ensayos* (Madrid: Revista de Occidente, 1944), pp. 11-35.
6. See Del Río, "Vida y obra," *Federico García Lorca,* p. 42.
7. Del Río, p. 57.
8. "Soneto de homenaje a Manuel de Falla, ofreciéndole unas flores," published by Eduardo Molina Fajardo in *La Estafeta Literaria,* No. 456 (15 November 1970), p. 5.
9. Molina, *Cante flamenco,* pp. 22-23.
10. This letter was published with the sonnet to Falla in Molina Fajardo's article, p. 6 (see note 8, above).
11. See W. H. Auden, *The Enchafèd Flood or the Romantic Iconography of the Sea* (London: Faber and Faber, 1951).
12. Couffon, *Granada y García Lorca,* p. 109.
13. Molina and Mairena, *Mundo y formas,* p. 292.
14. Manfredi Cano, *Geografía,* p. 157.
15. José Carlos de Luna, *De cante grande y cante chico* (Madrid: n.p., 1926), p. 112.
16. Quoted from Benjamín Jarnés in Campbell, *Lorca,* p. 30.
17. Campbell, *Lorca,* pp. 15-16.
18. Guillermo Díaz-Plaja, *Federico García Lorca* (Madrid: Espasa Calpe, 1961), p. 39.
19. There are exceptions, such as the elegies written for cities lost to other Islamic factions or to the Christians. See James T. Monroe, ed. and trans., *Hispano-Arabic Poetry: A Student Anthology* (Berkeley: University of California Press, 1974).
20. Molina, *Cante flamenco,* p. 136.
21. Lorca also discussed the Roman dualism of Cordova in his lecture on Góngora: "Góngora . . . seeks in the lonely air of Cordova the voices of Seneca and Lucan" (I:1004).
22. Molina and Mairena, *Mundo y formas,* p. 270.
23. Manfredi Cano, *Geografía,* p. 191.
24. D. E. Pohren, *The Art of Flamenco* (Jerez de la Frontera: Editorial Jerez Industrial, 1962), p. 137.

25. Molina and Mairena, *Mundo y formas,* p. 295.
26. Manfredi Cano, *Geografía,* p. 164.
27. Luna, *De cante grande y cante chico,* p. 111.
28. Molina, *Cante flamenco,* p. 32.
29. For example in the *Romancero gitano,* "Romance de la luna, luna" (I:393). See Ramos-Gil, *Claves líricas,* pp. 246-47.
30. Pedro Salinas, "Lorca and the Poetry of Death," in *Lorca,* (ed. Durán), p. 100.
31. Molina and Mairena, *Mundo y formas,* p. 297.
32. Compare the "Martirio de Santa Olalla," where the motif of female breasts on a tray also appears in a climate of Roman cruelty (I: 434).
33. Rubén Benítez, *Bécquer tradicionalista* (Madrid: Gredos, 1971), p. 197.
34. *Costumbrismo y novela* (Berkeley: University of California Press, 1956).
35. Díaz-Plaja, *Federico García Lorca,* pp. 32-33.

Chapter 6

1. Lafuente, *Los gitanos,* pp. 42-43.
2. From a letter to Jorge Guillén (II: 1137). The emphasis is Lorca's.
3. López-Morillas, "Lyrical Primitivism: García Lorca's *Romancero gitano,"* in *Lorca,* (ed. Durán), pp. 133-34.
4. *La poesía mítica,* p. 40.
5. Luis Rosales, "La Andalucía del llanto (Al margen del *Romanero gitano,"* *Cruz y Raya,* No. 14 (1934), p. 46.
6. Melchor Fernández Almagro, "Federico García Lorca: *Romancero gitano,"* *Revista de Occidente,* No. 21 (1928), pp. 373-78.
7. It is well known that the *siguiriya* is a close relative of the *playera* (*plañidera*), originally a song of mourning, as indicated by its name.
8. Clébert, *The Gypsies,* p. 234.
9. Arturo Barea, *Lorca: El poeta y su pueblo* (Buenos Aires: Losada, 1956), p. 73.
10. *The Gypsies,* p. 230.
11. Machado y Álvarez, *Cantes flamencos,* p. 34.
12. Paul Sébillot, *Le Folk-lore de France* (1904; rpt. Paris: Maissonneuve et Larose, 1968).
13. Ramos-Gil, *Claves líricas,* pp. 208-16.
14. Among recent studies, see Virginia Higginbotham, "Lorca's Apprenticeship in Surrealism," *Romanic Review,* 61 (1970), 109-22; Paul Ilie, *The Surrealist Mode in Spanish Literature. An Interpretation of Basic Trends from Post-Romanticism to the Spanish Vanguard* (Ann Arbor: University of Michigan Press, 1968).
15. *Los gitanos,* p. 22.
16. Lafuente, p. 23.
17. Machado y Álvarez, *Cantes flamencos,* p. 62.
18. Del Río, "Vida y obra," pp. 37-38.
19. Lafuente, p. 23.
20. López-Morillas, "Lyrical Primitivism," p. 136.

Chapter 7

1. Adolfo Salazar, "La saeta," *Nuestra Música,* No. 21 (1951), p. 33.
2. Molina and Mairena, *Mundo y formas,* p. 255.
3. Antonio and Manuel Machado, *Obras completas* (Madrid: Plenitud, 1947), p. 1006.
4. Francisco Rodríguez Marín, *Cantos populares españoles* (Seville: F. Alvarez y Compañía, 1882-83), no. 6529.
5. Rodríguez Marín, no. 6519.
6. Aguilar y Tejera, *Saetas populares,* no. 679. This collection (cited in Chapter 3) is the most complete in existence. However, many of its examples are not strictly *saetas:* they fall under the heading of religious poetry in general (*coplas, villancicos,* etc.).
7. Molina and Mairena, *Mundo y formas,* p. 256.
8. Salinas, "Lorca and the Poetry of Death," in *Lorca,* (ed. Durán), p. 106.
9. "La saeta," *Anuario Musical,* 4 (1949), 121. This and Salazar's article are probably the best published to date on the *saeta.*
10. Medina Azara, " 'Cante jondo' y cantares sinagogales" (cited in Chapter 1). See also *Encyclopedia Judaica* (Jerusalem: Encyclopedia Judaica, 1971-72).
11. Larrea, "La saeta," p. 120.
12. Rodríguez Marín, *Cantos populares,* no. 6525.
13. Antonio Domínguez Ortiz, *Los conversos de origen judío después de la expulsión* (Madrid: Consejo Superior de Investigaciones Científicas, 1955), p. 399.
14. Aguilar y Tejera, *Saetas populares,* no. 934.
15. *Cancionero popular* (Madrid: Carlos Bailly-Bailliere, 1865), I: xxii-xxv. Aguilar y Tejera would suggest the same possibility much later.
16. "La saeta," p. 36.
17. Rodríguez Marín, *Cantos populares,* nos. 6534, 6522.
18. Aguilar y Tejera, *Saetas populares,* no. 210.
19. "La saeta," p. 128.
20. Aguilar y Tejera, *Saetas populares,* no. 600. This poem recalls the tradition of the Holy Grail. Like the *saeta,* the Grail legend may be a "composite between Christianity and the Nature Ritual." Jesse L. Weston, *From Ritual to Romance* (1920; rpt. New York: Doubleday, 1957), p. 205.
21. Sir James Frazer, *The Golden Bough* (1890-1915; rpt. Toronto: Macmillan, 1969), pp. 265ff.
22. Manfredi Cano, *Geografía,* p. 185.
23. Rodríguez Marín, *Cantos populares,* no. 6533.
24. Frazer, *The Golden Bough,* p. 405.
25. Weston, *Ritual to Romance,* p. 204.
26. *Duelo de la Virgen* (Madrid: Biblioteca de Autores Españoles, 1952), p. 134.
27. Keith Whinnom, "El origen de las composiciones religiosas del Siglo de Oro: Mendoza, Montesino y Román," *Revista de Filología Española,* 46 (July-December 1963), 284.
28. Whinnom, p. 284.
29. In passing, a "Franciscan" note in Lorca's youthful poetry should be pointed

out here—a certain tenderness and identification with flowers, animals, and insects. He knew the *Fioretti,* and refers obliquely to the saint in his lecture on *duende* (I: 1069). But it is a more literal, basic kind of Franciscanism that concerns us here.

30. *Estudios de literatura religiosa española* (Madrid: Afrodisio Aguado, 1964), p. 60.

31. Fray Íñigo de Mendoza, *Cancionero* (Madrid: Espasa Calpe, 1968), p. 211. This edition was prepared by Professor Julio Rodríguez-Puértolas, to whom I am indebted for his help on this chapter.

32. Rodríguez Marín, *Cantos populares,* no. 6519.

33. Aguilar y Tejera, *Saetas populares,* no. 310.

34. R. Foulché-Delbosc, *Cancionero castellano del siglo XV* (Madrid: Carlos Bailly-Bailliere, 1912-15), p. 164.

35. Mendoza, *Cancionero,* pp. 164, 194.

36. Zamora, for example, on Easter Sunday in the Plaza Mayor. The difference here is that Christ has already been resurrected.

37. Rodríguez Marín, *Cantos populares,* no. 6523.

38. Foulché-Delbosc, *Cancionero castellano,* p. 257.

39. *Estudios,* p. 77.

40. Until now this work was believed to contain the first reference to the *saeta.* (See Gerardo Diego, "Origen de la saeta," *Consigna,* 14 [June 1954], 34-36; the quotations in the text are from this article, p. 35.) However, Professor Joseph R. Jones discovered an earlier reference to the *saeta* in the Biblioteca Nacional, Madrid, as the final manuscript of this chapter was being prepared. The work in question is José de Barcia y Zambrana, *Despertador cristiano de sermones doctrinales sobre particulares asuntos* . . . (Granada, 1678). There is a mention of *saetas* in the prologue and a collection of these songs at the end of the book, which was reprinted many times. I am indebted to Professor Jones for his assistance.

41. Franciscans in Italy, such as Jacopone da Todi, had sung the *laude.* This song and the French *virelai* (*virolai*) show marked differences from the *saeta.*

42. Diego, "Origen de la saeta," p. 36.

43. Weston, *Ritual to Romance,* p. 48.

44. There are two photographs of a *guiñol* or puppet theater constructed by the poet in Lorca's *Obras completas* (I: XLIV).

45. She especially recalls "La Tarara" (I: 800). The poet's Lola and the protagonist of a play by Antonio and Manuel Machado—*La Lola se va a los Puertos*—were probably inspired by a famous *cantaora* of the nineteenth century. See Molina, *Cante flamenco,* p. 81.

46. "The Grail Castle is always situated in the close vicinity of water, either on or near the sea, or on the banks of an important river. . . . The presence of water, either sea, or river, is an important feature of the Adonic cult." Weston, *Ritual to Romance,* p. 51.

47. As in "Balada triste" (I: 27-28).

48. Rodríguez Marín, *Cantos populares,* no. 6470. See also Lorca's "Reyerta" (I: 398). J. M. Flys suggests that the Judean lily and the Spanish carnation epitomize the character, people, and religions of the two lands. *El lenguaje poético de Federico García Lorca* (Madrid: Gredos, 1955), p. 163.

Chapter 8

1. "Notas sobre el elemento tradicional en la obra de García Lorca," *Filología*, No. 1 (May-August 1949), pp. 340-41.

2. *Fables of Identity: Studies in Poetic Mythology* (New York: Harcourt, Brace and World, 1963), pp. 19-20.

3. I: 1068. That Lorca knew *The Birth of Tragedy from the Spirit of Music* is evident from this lecture.

A Selected Bibliography

This bibliography includes only works essential to my study. A more complete list of books and articles on Lorca can be consulted in Joseph L. Laurenti and Joseph Siracusa, *Federico García Lorca y su mundo: Ensayo de una bibliografía general* (Metuchen, N.J.: The Scarecrow Press, 1974); and the poet's *Obras completas,* 2 vols., 18th ed. (Madrid: Aguilar, 1973). All quotations from Lorca refer to this edition. For works on *cante jondo,* the indispensable starting points are Anselmo González Climent's *Bibliografía flamenca* (Madrid: Escelicer, 1965); and the same author's *Segunda bibliografía flamenca* (Málaga: El Guadalhorce, 1966), compiled in collaboration with José Blas Vega. The latter has also published a useful annotated bibliography, "Apuntes crítico-informativos para una bibliografía del flamenco," in *La Estafeta Literaria,* No. 456 (15 November 1970), pp. 16-20. This issue of the magazine is devoted to Lorca and *cante jondo.*

WORKS ON GARCÍA LORCA

Allen, Rupert C. *Symbolic World of Federico García Lorca.* Albuquerque: The University of New Mexico Press, 1972.

Alonso, Dámaso. "Federico García Lorca y la expresión de lo español." In *Poetas españoles contemporáneos.* Madrid: Gredos, 1958.

Bardi, Ubaldo. *Federico García Lorca: musicista, scenografo e direttore della Barraca.* Florence: Provincia di Firenze, 1978.

Barea, Arturo. *Lorca: El poeta y su pueblo.* Buenos Aires: Losada, 1956.

Campbell, Roy. *Lorca.* London, New Haven: Yale University Press, 1952.

Cirre, J. F. "El caballo y el toro en la poesía de García Lorca." *Cuadernos Americanos,* No. 6 (November-December 1952), pp. 243-45.

Correa, Gustavo. *La poesía mítica de Federico García Lorca.* Madrid: Gredos, 1970.

Couffon, Claude. *Granada y García Lorca.* Buenos Aires: Losada, 1967.

Crow, John A. *Federico García Lorca.* Los Angeles: University of California Press, 1945.

Devoto, Daniel. "Notas sobre el elemento tradicional en la obra de García Lorca." *Filología,* No. 1 (May-August 1949), pp. 292-341.

Díaz-Plaja, Guillermo. *Federico García Lorca.* Madrid: Espasa Calpe, 1961.

Durán, Manuel, ed. *Lorca: A Collection of Critical Essays.* Englewood Cliffs, N.J.: Prentice-Hall, 1962. (Contains listed articles by Juan López-Morillas and Pedro Salinas.)

Eich, Christoph. *Federico García Lorca: Poeta de la intensidad.* Madrid: Gredos, 1970.

Fernández Almagro, Melchor. "Federico García Lorca: *Romancero gitano.*" *Revista de Occidente,* No. 21 (1928), pp. 373-78.

Flys, J. M. *El lenguaje poético de Federico García Lorca.* Madrid: Gredos, 1955.

Guardia, A. de la. *García Lorca: Persona y creación.* Buenos Aires: Sur, 1949.

Higginbotham, Virginia. "Lorca's Apprenticeship in Surrealism." *Romanic Review,* 61 (1970), 109-22.

Ilie, Paul. *The Surrealist Mode in Spanish Literature: An Interpretation of Basic Trends from Post-Romanticism to the Spanish Vanguard.* Ann Arbor: University of Michigan Press, 1968. Spanish version, Madrid: Taurus, 1972.

Josephs, F. Allen. "Elementos taurinos en *Llanto por Ignacio Sánchez Mejías.*" *García Lorca Review,* 2 (1974), n. pag.

López-Morillas, Juan. "Lyrical Primitivism: García Lorca's *Romancero gitano.*" In *Lorca: A Collection of Critical Essays,* edited by Manuel Durán. Englewood Cliffs, N.J.: Prentice-Hall, 1962.

Mora Guarnido, José. *Federico García Lorca y su mundo.* Buenos Aires: Losada, 1958.

Moreno Villa, José. "Instantes musicales con García Lorca." *Revista Musical Mexicana,* No. 10 (21 May 1942), pp. 223-24; No. 11 (7 June 1942), pp. 245-46.

Onís, Federico de. "Lorca, folklorista." In *Federico García Lorca (1899-1936).* See entry under Del Río, Ángel.

Ramos-Gil, Carlos. *Claves líricas de García Lorca: Ensayos sobre la expresión y los climas poéticos lorquianos.* Madrid: Aguilar, 1967.

Río, Ángel del. "Vida y obra." In *Federico García Lorca (1899-1936):*

Vida y obra. Bibliografía. Antología. Obras inéditas. Música popular. New York: Hispanic Institute, 1941.

Rizzo, Gino L. "Poesía de Federico García Lorca y poesía popular." *Clavileño,* No. 36 (November-December 1955), pp. 44-51.

Rosales, Luis. "La Andalucía del llanto (Al margen del *Romancero gitano*)." *Cruz y Raya,* No. 14 (May 1934), pp. 39-70.

Salinas, Pedro. "Lorca and the Poetry of Death." In *Lorca: A Collection of Critical Essays,* edited by Manuel Durán. Englewood Cliffs, N.J.: Prentice-Hall, 1962.

WORKS ON *CANTE JONDO* AND RELATED SUBJECTS

Andrade de Silva, Tomás. "Sobre los orígenes de treinta y tres cantes." *Antología del cante jondo* (recorded anthology). Madrid: Hispavox, 1958.

Caballero Bonald, José María. *Luces y sombras del flamenco.* Barcelona: Lumen, 1975.

Chase, Gilbert. *The Music of Spain.* 1941. Reprint. New York: Dover, 1959.

Clébert, Jean-Paul. *The Gypsies.* Baltimore: Penguin, 1969.

Falla, Manuel de. "Il canto primitivo andaluso (cante jondo)." *La Rassegna Musicale,* No. 10 (October 1938), pp. 357-67.

García Matos, Manuel. "Cante flamenco: Algunos de sus presuntos orígenes." *Anuario Musical,* 5 (1950), 97-124.

González Climent, Anselmo. *Flamencología: Toros, cante y baile.* Madrid: Escelicer, 1964.

————. "Para un historiografía flamenca." *Cuadernos Hispano-americanos,* No. 184 (April 1965), pp. 85-119.

Grunfeld, Frederick V. *The Art and Times of the Guitar: An Illustrated History of Guitars and Guitarists.* New York: Macmillan, 1970.

Lafuente, Rafael. *Los gitanos, el flamenco y los flamencos.* Barcelona: Barna, 1955.

Larrea, Arcadio de. "La saeta." *Anuario Musical,* 4 (1949), 105-35.

Luna, José Carlos de. *De cante grande y cante chico.* Madrid: n.p., 1926.

Machado y Álvarez, Antonio. *Cantes flamencos.* 1881. Reprint. Buenos Aires: Espasa Calpe, 1947.

Manfredi Cano, Domingo. *Geografía del cante jondo.* Madrid: Grifón, 1955.

Medina Azara (Máximo José Kahn). " 'Cante jondo' y cantares sinagogales." *Revista de Occidente,* 8 (October 1930), 53-84.

Molina, Ricardo. *Cante flamenco.* Madrid: Taurus, 1965.

Molina, Ricardo, and Mairena, Antonio. *Mundo y formas del cante flamenco.* Madrid: Revista de Occidente, 1963.

Molina Fajardo, Eduardo. *Manuel de Falla y el cante jondo.* Granada: Universidad de Granada, 1962.

Pemartín, Julián. *El cante flamenco: Guía alfabética.* Madrid: Afrodisio Aguado, 1966.

Rossy, Hipólito. *Teoría del cante jondo.* Barcelona: Credsa, 1966.

Salazar, Adolfo. "La saeta." *Nuestra Música,* No. 21 (1951), pp. 29-41.

Starkie, Walter. "Cante Jondo, Flamenco and the Guitar." *Guitar Review,* No. 20 (1956), pp. 3-14.

Tanno, John W. *Bibliography and Discography of Flamenco* (in progress).

Index

The works, lectures, poetry, and sketches of García Lorca are listed under his name. Individual poems are listed under the respective volume.